9/6/02

Heavenly Gaits: The Complete Guide to Gaited Riding Horses

Also by Brenda Imus:
From the Ground Up

Heavenly Gaits

The Complete Guide to
Gaited Riding Horses

By Brenda Imus

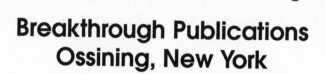

Breakthrough Publications
Ossining, New York

For information address:
Breakthrough Publications, Inc.
310 N. Highland Avenue
Ossining, New York 10562
www.booksonhorses.com

ISBN: 914327-82-5

Cover Photo: Owner Karen Swerdon on her spotted saddle horse stallion, Odd Man. Odd Man is performing a comfortable fox trot. He makes his home at Razzberry Hill Farm in New York.

03 02 01 00 99 98
9 8 7 6 5 4

*This book is whole-heartedly dedicated
to the One who makes a way
where there is no way,
and to the continued prosperity
of His marvelous creation:
the gaited horse.*

Table of Contents

—Acknowledgments—

Like most major publishing projects, this book has been the result of the cooperation of many individuals drawn together for a common purpose. Our common purpose was to give our gaited horses the attention they deserve, and to offer those interested in these types of riding animals (is there any *other* kind?) a thorough look at what the gaited horse world has to offer.

Much of the material herein has never before been published, but was gleaned from interviews and conversations with dozens of knowledgeable breed representatives. This work could only have come about as the result of the cooperation of many people who were willing to offer their time, suggestions, expertise and photographs, and I owe every one of them a debt of gratitude.

I thank Lynn Weatherman, Editor of *The American Saddlebred*, for his patient responses to my inquiries, and for providing photos of several important Saddlebred horses. Though he bills himself as my "toughest critic," as an *honest* and *fair* critic, his aid in this work was invaluable.

Mr. Verne Albright proved tremendously helpful by providing me with reams of material on his beloved Peruvian Paso, and by helping to "connect" me with others involved with that breed. Ann Elwell of the U.S. Icelandic Horse Federation not only provided me with excellent resource material and photos, but invited me to visit her farm so that I could experience the remarkable Icelandic Horse for myself. Rosalie MacWilliam helped ensure that none of the inaccuracies and errors about the Paso Fino that have commonly made their way into print found their way into this work. Janet Esther allowed me to borrow from her expertise regarding the Missouri Fox Trotting horse, and Lou Pitts of the Tennessee Walking Horse Breeders' and Exhibitors' Association responded to my requests promptly with helpful literature and illustrations.

Besides providing me with resources, information and illustrations, each of the above individuals proofread the chapter regarding their breed of horse, to help ensure that the information in this book is up-to-date, thorough and accurate. This is not to say that any information was *censored* by breed association people. On the contrary, there are a few instances (very few) where there were honest differences of opinion, or a desire existed to downplay certain historical facts. In each case, differences were handled graciously, and I was permitted to make editorial decisions based on all the information at hand. For people whose lives and reputations are wrapped up in these horses, that is no small concession. Perhaps over time the weight of evidence will shift, and I will be modifying a later edition to fall more in line with their views.

I want to thank Barbara Bouray of the North American Single-footing Horse Association and her husband, Dan Bouray, for providing me with several excellent photos, information and help. Sharon Major of *Horsetrend Magazine*, and Virginia Reames of *Favorite Gait* were also generous in their contributions. A special thanks goes to professional equine photographer Terry A. Walker and her husband Rex, of Terex Images, for their photos of Missouri Fox Trotting Horses. Mickey Anderson also donated many outstanding photos of Tennessee Walking Horses.

There are hardly words enough to express my appreciation to Leon Sargent, the world's premiere professional photographer of American Saddlebred horses. He was unbelievably generous in his contributions, and I can only say that I wish I were publishing two *more* books so that I could share with my readers more of the outstanding photographs that he made available to me. Thank you, Mr. Sargent—I only hope this work does *your* work justice.

Dr. Deb Bennet of the Equine Studies Institute was also helpful. Our initial telephone conversation helped get me started on the "right track," and when a serious question arose as to the accuracy of some important resource information, I contacted her, knowing that there are few, if any, more knowledgeable horse experts in the world who can offer reliable, definitive answers to sticky questions.

Many good friends gave me help and encouragement. I want to thank Ann Bell, Amy Jose and Brenda Carlson. Karen Swerdon spared a day from her busy schedule to allow me to photograph her and her Spotted Saddle Horse stallion, Odd Man, for the cover of this book. A grateful literary hug goes to my three children who were still at home—at least part of the time—while this work progressed. This book has been three long years in the making! Charlie, Zack and Jamie more than pulled their own weight around our home during that time. Thanks kids. (Who knows—maybe we can raise your allowances now!) My husband, Hugh, deserves the "husband of the decade" award for his patience and support. When things got rocky, he helped smooth the way.

My greatest thanks, and all the glory, goes to my Lord and Savior, Jesus Christ. He is the one Who made this all possible, and worthwhile. He is the one who opens doors that no man may close. Thank you, Jesus.

— FOREWORD —

Several years ago I participated in a large organized trail ride. The first day out I occasionally found myself in the company of a personable young man mounted on a lovely, large chestnut mare. Though there were nearly two hundred fit horses and experienced horsemen on that ride, this pair stood out from all the others. This fellow and his horse zig-zagged quickly and effortlessly through the roughest parts of the densely wooded trail like dancers performing an intricate ballet, while the rest of us, mounted on typical stock type horses, picked our way cautiously along. The duo moved out to the side of the line—often altogether off-trail—and zipped smoothly on ahead to keep company with the lead riders.Then they would wend their way back along the procession of trail horses and riders, stopping to visit along the way.

I realized there was something special about this man's horse, but assumed her speed, sure-footedness and beautiful way of going could largely be attributed to her rider's exceptional horsemanship abilities and the obvious rapport that existed between them. When I complimented him on these he just gave an embarrassed laugh, insisting that the horse was special not because of him, but because of her breeding and distinctive gait. She was a Missouri Fox Trotter.

We rode for over seven hours on the first day of that ride. As the riders came back into camp, a chorus of moans and groans was loosed over the countryside as saddle-sore *derrieres'* disengaged from saddles. Mine was no exception. Though I ride often, and my Appaloosa mare's walk, trot and canter is as smooth as most, my body protested vehemently at the day-long abuse heaped upon it. My poor horse was also pooped out.

We were all put to shame by the fellow with the fox trotter. Though they'd covered far more ground that day than any of us, he sprang lightly out of the saddle and gallantly volunteered to carry water buckets that I and my equally saddle-sore friend were staggering through the campgrounds with. I accepted his offer and asked if he wasn't exhausted from the long and difficult ride. He cheerfully asserted that the smooth gait of his horse was so easy to ride that he'd be happy to ride for another seven hours. He explained that his mare was also still fresh because she hadn't had to put up with his bouncing off her back to an uncomfortable trot all day. To prove his point, he offered to let me ride his fox trotter.

I wish I could say that I accepted his generous invitation, rode the mare, and have been hooked on gaited horses ever since. But the truth is, my prime interests at the time were in a hot shower, some hot food and a warm bed. My body was so stiff and sore that I couldn't bring myself to *think* about mounting and riding another horse that day. Though I missed that opportunity to sit a gaited horse, the impression that she made on me was lasting, and I was left with a desire to learn more about fox trotters.

Shortly after this I went trail-riding with a friend. The horse she made available to me was a nondescript, ancient flea-bitten Appaloosa who stood barely over fourteen hands high, and was nearly as wide as she was tall. At first I was embarrassed to be seen on such a horse. My poor opinion of this mare quickly changed to one of respect. She didn't have a lick of trot in her, but traveled along with what was by far the quickest, smoothest riding gait I'd ever sat. We skimmed along as though on greased ball bearings, rather than legs. This sure-footed, common-looking mare easily left other taller, younger and flashier horses eating her dust—and in spite of her age and diminutive size, she could go all day without tiring. I learned that her distinctive smooth gait is called the single-foot, and is known for being easy on both horse and rider. Again I was intrigued.

Shortly after riding the gaited Appaloosa I began to search for a trail horse for my husband Hugh. He wanted a tall, easy-going, comfortable horse. We hunted around for nearly a year with no luck. Then one day I accompanied a friend who went to examine a Tennessee Walking Horse. I took a turn in the saddle, and was thrilled with the long stride but smooth gait of this big horse. When my friend decided not to purchase the Walker, who was aptly called Fancy, I talked Hugh into going back to the farm with me "just to look." The asking price was nearly twice what we planned to spend.

Nevertheless, we left the farm that day the proud new owners of a registered Tennessee Walking Horse, and have never once regretted our decision to buy her. Fancy is by far the most stylish and spirited horse in our small barn. Despite her bold willingness, she's remarkably kind, obedient, and easy to ride.

While I had been mildly intrigued by gaited horses before, now I was seriously interested. As I gained first-hand experience working with Fancy, I kept hearing more and more wonderful things about other breeds of gaited horses from friends and acquaintances. Many of the horse people I respected most were committed owners, and promoters, of gaited horses. By now I was a convert, and knew that any future horse purchases would surely be of gaited stock. With this in mind, I attempted to learn as much as I could about these special horses.

Some kinds of information were easy to come by. I soon learned that gaited horses of every description are rapidly increasing in number. During a period when the U.S. horse industry as a whole saw a slump in the number of newly registered horses, registration figures demonstrate a dramatic increase in the population of gaited horse breeds. The number of newly registered Paso Finos increased by more than 33% between 1990 and 1993. During that time there was approximately a 20% increase in registered Missouri Fox Trotters and Peruvian Pasos. There are nearly 300,000 registered Tennessee Walking Horses in this country; a number that is also rising.

The burgeoning interest in gaited breeds is not limited to the United States. Germany, for example, is home to more than 60,000 Icelandic horses—a hardy gaited breed that has only been exported from its native Iceland since the mid-1950's.

Besides the increase in numbers of established breeds, the past few years have seen the establishment of several new gaited horse registries. The National Spotted Saddle Horse Association was founded in 1979, the Walkaloosa became a recognized breed in 1985, the Rocky Mountain Horse Association was established in 1986, the U.S. Icelandic Horse Federation began taking registries in 1988, the Mountain Pleasure Horse Association was formed in 1989, the North American Single-Footing Horse Association opened its books in 1990, and the Tiger Horse Association in 1994. Another relative newcomer is the registered Racking Horse; a registry that has grown to 70,000 since its inception in 1971. Besides these, there are a number of horse breeds with a distinct *inclination* for the lateral gaits, but who also number trotting horses among them. Such are the Florida Cracker Horse and the McCurdy horses.

Despite this burgeoning interest, I couldn't find a single authoritative source of information on the gaited horse, *per se*. I discovered magazine articles that promoted one breed or another, but this information was usually more sketchy and anecdotal than what I was looking for. While there are books available that give a very brief overview of many breeds of horses and a few books that relate specifically to one or another gaited breed, I wanted something that would give me a thorough overall view of each major type of gaited horse. After several trips to the library and a giant raid of my friends' equestrian bookshelves I finally realized there was no such book. This seemed like an unbelievable gap in the equestrian book world.

At this time I'd recently completed my first book, *From the Ground Up*, and was primed for a new project. I was already deeply involved in researching the gaited horse breeds, and now had some personal experience with the Tennessee Walking Horse. It seemed only logical to pull as much printed research information together as possible, visit and correspond with owners and trainers directly involved with these breeds, acquire the help and cooperation of the gaited breed horse associations, and write a book for others who needed the same kind of information I'd been seeking.

I decided this book would offer an historical background on each breed of gaited horse. Though this might seem like a lot of extraneous information, to know a breed's background is to know the breed. These sections include information about foundation stock and influential individual horses and trainers within each breed. It also seemed important to describe and show the ideal conformation of each horse, and explain why certain physical characteristics are considered desirable. I have also attempted to clearly describe each breed's unique temperamental qualities, point out common problems, and outline training and handling methods commonly employed with them.

Perhaps most importantly, I have tried to convey to the reader how it actually feels to ride a typical horse of each breed. This latter can be done partly—but only in part —through charts showing the order of footfalls of various gaits, and by description. Description and illustration, however, will never do these horses justice. It is my earnest hope that those of you interested in gaited horses make every attempt to ride as many kinds of these wonderful animals as possible. This is especially true if you are considering entering the realm of gaited horse owner, either for the first time, or as an expansion of an existing interest.

My research confirmed my early impressions about gaited horses. They are a lovely and special presence in this world. It's been a privilege to become so closely associated with them, and with so many people dedicated to their continued prosperity.

Two types of gaited horses, originating from different parts of the world. Top, the "Colonial," or Spanish, type of gaited horse. Below, the English type.

-- INTRODUCTION --

EARLY GAITED HORSES

No detailed ancient history of the gaited horse comes down to us from ancient times. Writers of those eras seldom made a distinction between ambling horses and trotting horses, while artists, rather than representing their subject accurately, often depicted the horse performing an impossible leaping gait.

Yet we do have a small but convincing body of extant written and artistic evidence that gaited saddle horses have been used and valued since antiquity. Early Roman documents refer to the gaited horse as a *gradarious* or *ambulator* (one with a variable walk, or walker) and to the trotting horse as a *cussator* or *cruciator* (tormentor or crucifier). Two famous equestrian statues of the Renaissance — the Gattamelata by Donatello in Padua and the statue of Bartolemeo Colleoni by Verocchio in Venice—depict horses being ridden at the amble. Amblers are also depicted in other Renaissance-era art: *bas* reliefs, frescos, miniatures, mosaics and paintings. Such evidence indicates that gaited, or ambling, riding horses were familiar in Western Europe from the Middle Ages to the seventeenth century.

Spain enjoyed a strong tradition of horsemanship, and Granada produced the rather plain-looking but smooth-moving Spanish Jennet (pronounced *Janay'*). Starting about 800 AD Spain began importing the Barb (or Berber) from the Barbary Coast of North Africa. The Barb is a muscular,

7

compact horse known for its flowing mane and tail as well as for its smooth lateral riding gaits. This horse was extensively crossed with native Spanish stock—and some claim with Arabian horses as well—eventually leading to the creation of the Andalusian and the Spanish Barb. Because of the Spanish Barb's North African Barb lineage, many horses of this breeding were able to perform saddle gaits.

During the Middle Ages in England, some people rode a small ambling horse called a palfrey. These horses are referred to in Chaucer's *Canterbury Tales* (c. 1400), where he says of the Wife of Bath, "Upon an Amblere esily she sat," and of the Monk, "His palfrey was as broun as a berye."

The term *palfrey* didn't signify a particular breed but rather a generic type of saddle horse, much as we use the term "stock horse" in the U.S. today. The palfrey was generally a horse trained to cover ground at a comfortable ambling gait. This gait could be performed slowly, or at great speed.

Over time certain regions became known for specific types of palfreys. Ireland's palfreys, for example, were called *Hobbies*, while the type of saddle horse bred and trained for riding in Scotland was known as the *Galloway*. Besides these, lateral gaited ponies were native to the Shetland and Orkland Islands.

Palfreys such as the Hobbies and Galloways were the preferred mode of transportation for many years in the British Isles, while trotting horses were relegated to the rank of peasants' mounts or pack animals. Well-to-do people used palfreys for general travel, hunting and hawking (hunting small prey with the use of specially trained falcons).

Palfreys were the genteel person's horse. Only poor peasants rode "bone-shakers," or trotting horses. This is understandable since efficient riding techniques, such as posting the trot, were yet to be developed. Horseback riding was done strictly "by the seat of the pants." While this presented few problems to the person mounted on an easy-gaited palfrey, riding most trotting horses was uncomfortable. This surely held true for the horse as well as for the rider, since there was no such thing as riding "technique." Therefore, the rider's weight would have bounced off the hapless animal's back with every stride. As most horsemen can attest, a horse that's uncomfortable under saddle is likely to be stubborn and balky. So trotting horses tended to be uncomfortable, stubborn and balky, while the smooth little palfrey was appreciated for its kind and willing temperament, as well as for comfortable riding gaits.

Many factors helped bring an end to the widespread use of smooth-gaited horses. The sport of hunting with falcons declined. Horse racing became extremely popular in England during the latter 1600's, and trotting breeds were generally faster race horses. Eventually British Royalty began importing Arab, Barb and Turkish stallions to cross on native mares, thus creating the Thoroughbred and greatly expanding the genetic pool of trotting blood. People began to travel more by coach than astride, so that a horse's speed and strength—rather than comfortable gaits under saddle—became prime considerations. Sidesaddle design improved so that ladies could ride trotting horses, even over fences, with an acceptable measure of comfort and dignity.

During the seventeenth century "high school" equestrians in France and Austria were developing riding techniques that enabled riders to more comfortably ride the trot. The Andalusian—an important forebear to the Lippizaner—was a trotting breed created from crossing Barbs and Arabs with native stock. The Andalusian became the horse of choice for heads of state, wealthy landowners, powerful conquistadors, and anyone else who could afford to own one. All of these factors combined to help spell an end to the ambling horse tradition, and the start of the trotting horse's popularity.

The ambling/pacing horse tradition didn't die out altogether, however. In many regions of the world settled by Europeans before 1650—The New World, Iceland, South Africa, Northern Spain, Portuguese districts, the Caribbean Islands—descendants of the easy-gaited horses still flourished. Horsemen in these regions who appreciated the fine qualities of ambling/pacing horses continued to breed and improve upon them, thereby developing a number of ambling breeds.

The many distinct types and characteristics of modern gaited horses can be attributed to the fact that horsemen from different parts of the world used the types and breeds of gaited horses available to their region. These were crossed judiciously with high-quality imported and/or non-gaited horses, such as the Andalusian or Thoroughbred. Most of today's breeds of gaited horses owe a great debt to such distant cousins.

Climate, nutrition, geographical location and political considerations also played important roles in breed development. Where forage and domestic food supplies were scarce, horses tended to remain small. In regions of the world where food and forage was plentiful, horses grew larger. Countries that were geographically isolated—such as Peru and Iceland—tended quickly to produce animals that bred true to type, since importation of genetically diverse animals was difficult or impossible. In some cases political influences further impeded importation and/or cross breeding. These factors help explain why some horses possess very deep lineage and type, while other breeds show more disparity. Some breeds are being developed and refined up to the present day.

Regardless of the overall size, appearance or type of gaited breed, one genetic factor firmly embedded since ancient times predisposes the gaited, or ambling, horses of the world to one common characteristic: comfortable saddle gaits.

There is extant evidence that ambling horses have been with us for a very long time. Careful study shows that this example of ancient ice cave drawings, located in France, depicts a laterally-gaited horse.

–Chapter One–
The Gaits of a Horse

WHAT IS GAIT?

Actually all vertebrates, including man, may be said to have gaits. We can run, jog and walk. In addition, we may two-step, skip, and perform dance steps such as the rhumba or waltz. These are all different gaits. Each person has an individual way or style of performing these gaits. Besides this, we may perform them differently at various times. We may, in our own individual style, walk energetically forward, walk with a spring to our step, walk stiff-legged, walk as though marching, walk dispiritedly, drag our feet—the list goes on. Likewise we can perform our other gaits in varying ways. If all of this makes it seem like we two-legged humans possess an almost infinite repertoire of movement, imagine how much greater that repertoire would be if we, like the horse, possessed four legs rather than two!

The horse's gait may be described as his manner of moving, especially, but not exclusively, as it relates to the order of footfalls. Strictly speaking, all horses are gaited insofar as they all have *some* manner of moving across the ground.

But the term *gaited horse* has commonly come to mean horses that boast gaits other than the walk, trot and canter, the horse's three most common—or at least most well-known—gaits. Even more specifically, it refers to horses that use gaits alternate to the trot. These are referred to as *intermediate* gaits.

11

HEAVENLY GAITS

Because the horse possesses so many possible gaits, we need to break this subject into understandable components. The simplest, most common way this is done is to categorize most of the horse's gaits as either *lateral* or *diagonal*. That is, either the horse moves same-side (lateral) sets of legs in unison, or it moves diagonally opposed sets of legs in unison. To understand what constitutes a lateral or diagonal gait is to begin understanding what a gait really is.

PERFECT LATERAL/DIAGONAL GAITS

THE PACE

Lateral gaits are those where the horse's same side fore and hind legs move forward together; *ie*: left fore and hind, right fore and hind.

The purest example of a lateral gait is the *pace*, where the same side fore and hind legs move in synchrony and the lateral sets of feet land in perfect unison. The pace is a two-beat gait; that is, since the fore and hind feet on each side land at the same time, the two feet produce a single "beat" of sound. Also, there is a moment of suspension between the time the legs on one side lift from the ground and the legs of the opposite side set down. This creates a discernible space or unit of time between each beat. So the pace sounds like 1–2; 1–2. See graph number one, page 19.

THE TROT

Diagonal gaits are those in which the horse's legs at opposite corners, or diagonally opposed limbs, move forward in unison; *ie*: left hind and right fore; right hind and left fore.

The purest diagonal gait is the *trot*, where diagonal sets of legs move forward precisely together and the feet strike the ground in perfect unison. Like the pace, the trot is also a two-beat gait with a moment of suspension, or discernible space, making it sound like 1–2; 1–2. See graph number two, page 19.

WHAT DETERMINES GAIT

The timing of the hind legs as they relate to the motion of the forelegs determines whether a gait is lateral or diagonal. If the horse synchronizes same-side hind and fore legs, as in the pace, then the gait is lateral. If same-side fore and hind legs move in opposition to one another, as in the trot, the gait is diagonal. The changing relationship between hind and fore legs all along the spectrum between these two extremes is what creates the gaits unique to the gaited riding horse.

Not all horses are capable of fast lateral motion such as the pace. These horses—which constitute the majority—are strictly trotting horses. Those that can pace, or at least move their hind legs somewhat out-of-synch with the true diagonal trot, are capable of producing one or more of the specialized gaits. The more ability of motion the horse has along this spectrum, the more gaits he is capable of performing.

THE WALK

If you've ever casually observed a horse walking across a field and tried to ascertain the order of footfalls, you were likely frustrated in your endeavor due to the difficulty of keeping track of all those legs moving independently. One moment it may have appeared that the horse's hind leg contacted the ground just ahead of the same side fore—but then, no!—surely it was the fore foot that landed just before the opposite side hind. Just when did that front foot come off the ground, anyway? Somehow you missed something—better try again. Chances are, unless you were extremely determined, you quit trying to analyze the horse's walk.

But it's not hard to understand the walk once you learn how to look at it. The order of footfalls for the walk is: left hind, left front; right hind, right front. Simple, right? The walking gait only becomes confusing when you lose track of a leg and then begin observing the horse's walk at a point in the footfall sequence when a fore, rather than a hind, foot contacts the ground. Then the gait appears to be diagonal, and looks like this: left front, right hind; right front, left hind.

The timing of the footfalls in a good flat walk is even, so that each foot picks up and sets down independently. This makes the gait neither diagonal nor lateral, but "four cornered." Therefore the walk is an even 4-beat gait that sounds like this: 1-2-3-4. All of the intermediate gaits (those gaits that fall between the pace and trot) are actually variations of the walk. For this reason the French used to call the walk "the mother of gaits." See graph number three, page 19.

THE CANTER

At the *canter* two diagonal sets of legs move in unison while the other two corner legs move independently of one another. Therefore, the canter is neither a lateral nor a diagonal gait, though two legs do move with diagonal action. As the only three-beat gait, it falls into its own category.

At the canter a horse should move on either the left or right lead, depending upon his direction of travel. This means that when moving on a circle the horse moves the "leading," or inside, front and hind legs farther ahead than the non-leading pair in order to keep its balance. This is because a greater proportion of the horse's weight will be leaning toward the center of the circle.

On a right lead canter, the left hind leg is brought under the horse, and he uses it as a kind of "springboard" as he leaps forward, the other three feet off the ground. The right (leading) hind leg reaches deeply under the horse's body and lands on the ground in unison with the left fore leg, which leg balances and steadies the horse as it stretches it's right (leading) foreleg far forward. An instant after the right leading foreleg strikes the ground, the diagonally paired legs come up so that all of the horse's weight is borne on the leading front leg. This is the reason why many people call the inside front leg the leading leg—but actually it is the *inside hind leg* that provides the most forward impulsion. As the horse's body moves over the inside front leg the left hind sets down once more to help the horse spring forward, and the sequence is repeated.

The canter is a three beat gait with an extra measure of space between each set of footfalls, making it sound uneven, like this: 1-2-3--1-2-3--1-2-3. The order of footfalls at the right lead is: left hind; right hind and left front together; right front. The order is reversed when the horse is traveling on his left lead. See graphs numbers four and five, page 20.

THE GALLOP

The *gallop* is always done at speed with the horse stretched full-out, while the canter is a relatively slow collected gait. Otherwise, everything noted above about the order of footfalls at the canter is true of the gallop, with one important exception: at the gallop the two "paired" diagonal legs land out of synchrony, giving this gait a fast four-beat sound: 1 2 3 4 - 1 2 3 4. See graphs numbered six and seven, page 20.

SPECIAL GAITS

What causes some people to prefer gaited saddle horses to the trotting horse is the extra measure of comfort experienced by the rider. This is because there is no moment of suspension in the horse's gaits. Also the horse's back motion tends to be more forward and back and/or side to side than up and down, thereby reducing concussion between the horse's back and the rider's seat.

Because it is neither too fast, too slow, nor too collected, a non-gaited horse's best ground-covering working gait is usually the trot. But the trot's action creates an up-and-down motion in the back. This, combined with the impact caused by the horse's entire weight landing on the ground after suspension, makes the trot an extremely bouncy, jarring gait. Of course the rider can compensate for this by various means. He can post the trot by using his ankles, knees and hips as shock absorbers while cutting down the number of concussions between his seat and the saddle by standing in the stirrups every-other beat; he can teach his horse to shuffle along at a less bone-jarring jogging trot, keeping its feet close to the ground; he can learn to soften and relax his back and seat and sit the trot. No matter what, however, it requires patience, physical fitness and skill to ride the trot. No such special qualifications are required to comfortably ride a gaited saddle horse.

If the trot is difficult for a rider to master, the pace is nearly impossible. Besides the up-and-down action and the impact after suspension, the pace has a definite side-to-side swaying motion that can make a rider feel like he's being tossed around on stormy seas. Riding a fast pace can make even top-notch riders feel like seasick sailors.

Though the flat walk is limiting due to its slow speed, the faster smoother saddle gaits are little more than variations of the walk, with action sometimes being closer to the trot or pace. During intermediate saddle gaits the rear feet land out of synchrony with the front feet, thus reducing or eliminating suspension. The gaited horse's hind legs may also tend to glide, slide or shuffle forward, rather than land hard and square. These actions reduce concussion between horse and ground, which reduces jarring to the rider.

To elaborate: If the gait is nearly a pace, but the hind feet' timing is such that they contact the ground an instant before the front feet, then you have a *stepping pace*. If the gait is a walk, but performed so that the hind legs reach, or glide, much deeper under the horse than at the ordinary walk, and at much greater speed, then you have a *running walk*. If the gait is similar to a trot, but the timing of the legs' action causes each foreleg to land slightly ahead of the diagonally opposed hind leg, then you have a *fox trot*.

Another specialized gait is the *rack* which, like the walk and running walk, falls half-way between the two extremes of trot and pace. At the rack all four legs move independently of one another. A pure rack is, therefore, a square gait that is neither lateral nor diagonal. Few horses perform an absolutely pure rack. Usually the rack tends to fall toward either end of the lateral/diagonal spectrum: either it is slightly lateral and closer to a stepping pace, or slightly diagonal and closer to a fox trot. In the show ring, however, experienced judges look for the horse with purity of action, which is to say the horse who demonstrates no sign of paciness or trottiness at the rack.

The following is a detailed analysis of each of these gaits, and how various breeds of horses ideally perform them.

THE STEPPING PACE
(Slow Gait; Amble; Paso Fino; Sobreanado; Single-Foot)

Like the pace, the *stepping pace* is a lateral gait; two same-side sets of legs move in unison. In fact, the stepping pace is the same as the pace with one important exception: the hind leg strikes the ground an instant before the front leg, and the front leg either stays on the ground until the opposite hind leg has been set down, or is picked up a split second before. This eliminates the pace's period of suspension, making for a comfortable ride.

The stepping pace is also known as *slow gait*, and is one of the gaits utilized by five-gaited American Saddlebred show horses. When slow-gaiting, the horse's frame is condensed, or collected, his legs are lifted high and the gait is performed to a very slow cadence. This is lovely to watch but rather hard work for the horse. While the slow gait is considered artificial, in that it must be taught, not all horses are able to learn it. A horse must exhibit a natural inclination for lateral pace-like action in order to learn to slow gait. Some horses do exhibit a natural stepping pace—this is often noted in pacey horses when they are feeling excited or nervous.

The terms "amble" or "single-foot" are usually used to designate smooth-gaited trail and pleasure horses. In this variation of the stepping pace, one foot is on the ground at all times, and the "single-footing" horse seems to be moving along at a comfortable, easy amble. The low action, sliding, non-suspensory shuffling gait of the single-footing horse is comfortable for both horse and rider over all kinds of terrain and for extended periods of time. Indeed, some natural single-footing horses possess neither trot nor pace, but utilize the walk, amble and canter exclusively.

The stepping pace also forms the basis for some of the gaits of the Peruvian Paso and the Paso Fino. The low stepping pace and paso gaits are known for being comfortable over long distances for both horse and rider. The Paso Fino performs its show gait with very short strides.

The stepping pace's order of footfalls is: left hind; left front; right hind; right front. The stepping pace has an almost imperceptible unevenness to the rhythm: 1-2--3-4. See graph number eight, page 21.

THE FOX TROT (FOX WALK)

The *fox trot* is the gait closest to the trot, the main difference being that in the fox trot diagonally opposed feet do not land at the same time. The fore foot lands on the ground just prior to the diagonally opposed hind foot. Also, the fox trotter uses his powerful hind hocks as rear "springs," giving a fox trotting horse the appearance of being much lower behind than in front. This action softens the concussion between the horse and the ground, enabling the fox trotter to quickly cover many miles without unduly tiring himself or his rider. The *fox walk*, a term seldom used any more, is a very slow fox trot.

You may sometime hear the old adage that a fox trotter "walks in front and trots behind." This is impossible, of course, since a trot is the result of the relationship between the fore and hind legs. The impression of trottiness in back is caused by a moment of suspension that may occur between footfalls of the hind feet. Since there is no suspension in front, the forequarters appear to "walk."

The fox trot's footfalls are as follows: left hind; right fore; right hind; left fore. The shuffling action of the back feet produces a unique, uneven four-beat gait: 1--2-3--4. See graph number nine, page 21.

THE RACK
(Tolt, Flying Pace, Paso Llano, Paso Largo)

The *rack*, being neither lateral nor diagonal, falls directly between a trot and a pace. The order of footfalls at the rack is: left hind; left front; right hind; right front. Though this may sound like the walk or stepping pace (keeping in mind again that all special saddle gaits are actually variations of the walk), in execution it is different from either, as each leg and foot flashes quickly forward and sets down independently. For example, when a hind foot sets down, the opposite forefoot comes off the ground, while the other hind and its opposing forefoot are at the apex of their upward motion (moving in opposition to one another). So no two legs move in synchrony. The rack has a purely square, or even, 1-2-3-4 beat.

Five-gaited American Saddlebreds may perform the rack at blazing speeds. The rack as performed in the show ring is highly animated, and there is a moment of suspension between each footfall. While all of the energy produced by the animated foot and leg action is absorbed through the animal's body, thus making it a comfortable gait for the rider, a true animated rack is wearing on the horse, and should not be utilized for long periods.

The rack forms the basis for the *tolt*, the *flying pace*, the *paso llano*, and the *paso largo*. The differences among these gaits lie mostly in the way the individual horses, and breeds, carry their bodies. While the general carriage and silhouettes may vary, the gait is the same. It is a four-beat, four-cornered gait with the same order of footfalls as the walk, and shares the same even 1-2-3-4 beat, but with faster timing. See graph number eleven, page 21.

18

The Pace (#1)

The pace is a 2-beat *true lateral* gait, with same-side, or lateral, sets of legs moving together. Note that in (1), the right set of legs are forward, on the ground. As they push the horse forward, it's weight is centered over the right legs (2). There is a brief moment of suspension (3) just before both left legs land squarely together on the ground (4). Now the weight is carried on these legs as the horse moves forward (5); again, suspension (6), until the right legs touch the ground again (7), and the cycle is repeated (1).

The Trot (#2)

The trot is an even 2-beat *true diagonal* gait where diagonal sets of legs work together. In (1) the left front and right hind legs land together, carry the horse forward (2) and then are lifted for a moment of suspension (3) before the right front/left hind strike the ground together. It is the concussion upon landing from the moment of suspension that causes the trot to be "bone jarring" to some extent. The horse's weight is now carried by the right front/left hind diagonal (5), then another moment of suspension (6), and the original cycle begins again (7).

The Flat Walk (#3)

The flat walk falls between the lateral/diagonal spectrum, and is a *square gait*. The sequence is: left hind, left front (1) (with right front picking up), body carried forward on left lateral (2), right hind, right front (3) (with left front picking up), body carried on right lateral. Repeat cycle (1).

- ● *Weight-bearing foot, solidly on ground*
- ○ *Foot off ground*
- ▨ *Foot coming forward, touching ground*
- ⊙ *Foot back, still touching ground*

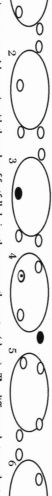

- ● *Weight-bearing foot, solidly on ground*
- ○ *Foot off ground*
- ◓ *Foot coming down, touching ground*
- ◉ *Foot back, still touching ground.*

The Canter, right lead (#4)

The canter is the only **3-beat** gait. The right lead canter begins as the horse brings its left hind/right front diagonal (1) and uses it to spring forward onto the right hind/left front diagonal (2). The horse pushes off from this diagonal onto its right front (3). There is a period of suspension (4) then the left hind comes under to repeat the cycle.

The Canter, left lead (#5)

The left lead canter begins as the horse brings its right hind under its body (1) and uses it to spring forward onto the left hind/right front diagonal (2). The horse pushes off from this diagonal onto its left front (3); a period of suspension (4), and the cycle is repeated by the hind, rather than the fore, leg, with the leading hind leg reaching very deeply under horse and landing in synchrony with the front diagonal.

The Gallop, right lead (#6)

The gallop is an uneven 4-beat gait, with the order of footfalls being the same as the canter (above). The difference between the two is that each foot lands independently. There are several periods of suspension between footfalls (2, 5). There is another period of suspension between (6) and (1), as the cycle is repeated.

The Gallop, left lead (#7)

The left-lead gallop is a mirror-image of the right lead gallop. Right hind (1), suspension (2), left leading leg (3), right front (4), suspension (5), left front (6), suspension (not shown), then right hind (1).

The Stepping Pace (#8)

The stepping pace is a *modified lateral* gait, with same-side legs working together. The order of footfalls shown here is: right hind, right front (1); the horse's body is carried forward over these (2), then left hind, left front, as the right front lifts (3). The body is carried over these (4), and the cycle repeats itself (1).

The Fox Trot (#9)

The fox trot is a *modified diagonal* gait. The left front strikes just ahead of the right hind (1). These carry the horse forward as the right front and left hind move forward (2). There may be a moment of rear suspension as the right front strikes (3) just ahead of the left hind (4). These carry the horse forward (5) to the next cycle (1).

The Running Walk (#10)

The best running walk is neither lateral nor diagonal, but falls between the spectrum and is considered a *square* gait. The left front strikes as the right front is coming up (1), then the left front comes down (2), and the horse is carried forward on the left lateral (3). The right hind reaches deeply under the horse and sets down (4). The horse is carried forward on this diagonal (5), until the right front sets down (6). Note how deeply the horse reaches under itself within its hind legs.

The Rack (#11)

The rack is also a *square* gait. It is, in fact, very similar to the running walk, except that the rear foot does not overstride the front foot, there is no "head nod", and the overall leg and foot action is generally faster.

● *Weight-bearing foot, solidly on ground*

○ *Foot off ground*

▨ *Foot coming down, touching ground*

◉ *Foot back, still touching ground.*

(Arrows indicate sets of feet working together.)

*Above, Odd Man demonstrates the stepping pace, or amble. This is an intermediate lateral gait. Note how his front/back legs on either side are moving together, but not quite in unison. The hind leg sets down slightly before the same-side fore leg. **Below:** The fox trot, an intermediate diagonal gait. Note diagonal legs move together. Again, legs aren't quite in unison. The fore leg sets down slightly before the diagonally opposed hind leg.*

*The square intermediate gaits. **Above**, a lovely natural running walk. Note how diagonal legs are in perfect opposition to one another. This is the hallmark of a good square gait. **Below**, The Rabbit (Kenny Smith up) performs a perfect rack.*

23

THE RUNNING WALK

As stated above, the *running walk* is very similar to the rack—and also to the walk—but there are several factors that distinguish it from these other gaits. For one thing the rear quarters of a walking horse give him the ability to reach deeply underneath himself with every stride. The back feet may, in fact, naturally overstride the print (or *track*) of the forefoot by as much as 24 inches. ("Big Lick" Tennessee Walking Show Horses can be trained to overstride even more with the use of special training devices and techniques.) This overstriding action gives the walking horse tremendous forward impulsion at the walk.

A walking horse with good natural action relaxes and rounds his croup, back and neck (bascules). He also energetically nods his head with every stride, thereby utilizing and absorbing much of the energy created by his powerful hind quarters. The depth of the head nod is one way of telling how well a horse is performing its gait. This way of going, combined with the shock-absorbing nature of the horse's hock makeup and action, usually causes the rider to feel as though he is effortlessly straddling and guiding the energy of a ton of dynamite—which he very nearly is!

While the fox trotter is said to "walk in front and trot behind," just the opposite illusion is given with the walking horse. A horse performing the running walk may exhibit a moment of suspension in front, and none behind. See graph number ten, page 21.

STYLES OF MOTION

While the above are accurate descriptions of the various gaits, each horse will perform its gaits in his or her own inimitable style. For this reason, it's not true that all walking horses are "smooth as glass," nor do all fox trotters have the natural ability to "canter all day in the shade of a tree." Usually, however, even horses with very little refinement of motion can be taught to utilize their bodies more efficiently, thus improving their gaits and making them more comfortable to ride.

Often there are particular strengths and weaknesses unique to each breed or type of gaited riding horse. Some of the more common of these are described in this work, along with various training methods and riding techniques generally used, or recommended, by knowledgeable trainers. These will enable the person interested in owning and/or working with gaited saddle horses to help his horses move correctly and with efficiency and grace of motion.

GAITS ARE GENETICALLY DETERMINED

It should be noted here that the basis for most gaited breed differentiation lies in each breed's genetically determined ability—or proclivity—to perform certain gaits in a particular manner. The tendency to be gaited a certain way is determined both by the nervous system ("wiring") of the horse, and by its conformation, or mechanical ability to produce certain moves.

If a sire and dam are both strictly trotting horses, their offspring will be wired and built to trot. Likewise, two strong pacing horses will produce a pacer. On the other hand, if we breed a strong-gaited trotting mare to a strong-gaited pacing stallion, we'll have varying results with each match. Depending upon the prepotency and genetic makeup of the individuals, a percentage of their offspring will only trot (probably the highest percentage, since a trot breeds stronger than a pace), while others will only pace. The remainder will fall somewhere on the spectrum between the two gaits -- they'll tend toward the amble, running walk, or fox trot. A few will be able to both trot and pace. Those horses which "swings both ways" will possess the greatest range of, or potential for, gaited motion.

Now let's imagine we repeatedly breed a "swings both ways" stallion to a strong trotting mare. Some of the offspring will inherit their dam's strong tendency to trot, some their sire's ability to amble. Of the amblers, the gait many will prefer will be closer to their dam's trot than to the true pace, which strong gait is genetically removed by one full generation. (That's not to say it wouldn't be possible for a true pace to show up in this, or succeeding, generations).

Some of the offspring mentioned above will possess their dam's tendency toward diagonal (trotting) motion, tempered by their sire's lateral gait tendencies. Such a horse will demonstrate a trot that is slightly out of synch—a "weak" trot, which is a strong fox trot. If we breed this first generation fox trotting animal to another first generation fox trotter, at least some of the resulting foals should be able to fox trot. If this second-generation fox trotting horse is bred to another second generation fox trotting horse, the resultant foal will possess an even stronger genetic tendency to perform the fox trot. As this genetic trait becomes more fixed, or "locked in," through several generations of selective breeding, horses with a very strong fox trot gait will result. After several generations of breeding strictly fox trotting horses, the gait becomes such a dominant genetic characteristic that it will be passed on to 100% of the offspring. We've developed, in essence, a distinct type of gaited horse.

It is only within this writer's scope to write about general heritable gait tendencies. For a more thorough, and expert, treatment of heritable tendencies in gaited horses, see Appendix I.

A well-established gaited horse breed is seldom determined and judged merely by gait tendencies. Horses who consistently produce a particular gait will share similar conformations, colorations and temperaments—and these criteria also become instrumental in the selection of breeding stock. So while a Tennessee Walking Horse (again, for example) is genetically wired and built to produce the running walk, it also is coded for a noble head, laid-back shoulder, sure-footedness, and a sensible temperament.

TRAINING DEVICES AND GAIT

There will be a variance in the quality of gaits among animals that are genetically coded to produce a running walk (for example). One horse may be so strongly coded for the running walk that it is virtually impossible to throw him off his gait. Another may perform the running walk, but not with reliability. Such a horse may occasionally slip into a pace, another might tend to fall into a stepping pace (amble) or fox-trot.

It's possible using weighted, padded or wedged shoes and other types of mechanical or chemical training devices to strengthen such a weak-gaited horse's tendency to perform a correct running walk. These devices help change the timing of the horse's motion, while also conditioning the horse's body—and "muscle memory"—in such a way that it becomes physically easier for him to perform his gait. Some such techniques and devices are very useful in the hands of a knowledgeable, conscientious horse trainer.

It should be apparent, however, that if our goal is to improve and strengthen the gaited characteristics of a breed, such weakly gaited horses are a poor choice for breeding stock. We ought to be breeding the animal that demonstrates a strong natural tendency to perform its gait.

But not everyone who works with gaited horses is acting upon sound principles, or even out of a good conscience. Unfortunately, this holds equally true for horse show judges. Some horse show judges rate a horse according to false or exaggerated motion and/or a wild-looking eye, rather than on conformity to breed type, trueness of gait, beauty and presence. When this happens consistently, then trainers begin to use devices—and sometimes inhumane techniques—to produce winning gaited show horses. These man-made marvels of the show ring, though not possessing the ideal genetic makeup for their breed—in fact such a horse may be the antithesis of the ideal horse for that breed—nevertheless become the most celebrated, popular sires and dams for the next generation.

This is unfortunate, as many generations of selective breeding have gone into producing horses who will consistently produce a particular saddle gait. The result of artificial show standards is the genetic decline of a breed of horses that took knowledgeable, dedicated horsemen many generations to develop and refine.

THE HORSEMAN'S RESPONSIBILITY

It is not my intention here to teach the reader all he or she needs to know to become a horse breeder or trainer—not that such a thing would be possible in any case. I go into this subject only because it is the horseman's responsibility not to contribute in any way to the genetic decline of a breed. This means we need to learn to recognize a genuinely superior animal, to promote such animals, and to breed only the best to the best. We must not allow ourselves to be unduly influenced by the show ring fashion or styles of the day, but should always consider the breed's best long-range interests, and allow our actions to be dictated by these principles.

Such highly-principled, conscientious individuals were instrumental in developing the fine qualities of the various gaited horse breeds. The future welfare of these animals continues to rest with these kinds of independent thinkers.

— Chapter Two —
The American Saddlebred

CADILLAC OF HORSES

Many horse fanciers consider the American Saddlebred horse to be the epitome of equine power, grace, beauty and versatility—in American vernacular, the "Cadillac of horses." The breed has surely earned such accolades. Though it's inherent beauty and grace has caused it to become the world's premier show horse, the American Saddlebred is far more than merely the peacock of the equine world. This breed has successfully proved itself over fences, in the farmer's fields, as a calvary mount, on the trail, in the dressage ring, and in front of a carriage. Several American Saddlebreds have even become famous American movie stars!

It's little wonder this horse is so well-liked and versatile, as its history is one of close association with people, and of quick adaption to the needs of those people.

HISTORY OF "THE AMERICAN HORSE"

THE NARRAGANSETT PACER
In the mid-1600's English Colonists imported *Galloways* and *Hobbies*, gaited horses originating from Scotland and Ireland, respectively. Horse breeders from Virginia and the Narragansett Bay area of Rhode Island were

especially successful at selectively breeding these English pacers. It is surmised their success was due to the geography of their land. Herds of horses could be kept isolated on islets that jutted into the Atlantic ocean. These islets were easily fenced off to eliminate unwanted breeding animals from the herds.

By 1650 these colonists had created a consistent type of good saddle horse that became known as the Narragansett Pacer. The Narragansett Pacer was a well-muscled, short-coupled little horse possessed of great strength and endurance. Usually sorrel in color, under 14 hands, and rather plain in appearance, this horse was much sought after as a lady's mount thanks to its docile temperament and extremely easy riding gaits. Before long the Narragansett Pacer became one of the most popular horses in the English Colonies. It is reputed that Paul Revere took his famous ride on the back of a Narragansett Pacer.

Despite this early American gaited horse's popularity, the enterprising Colonists continued to devise ways to improve their horse stock. In 1706 Colonists began importing Thoroughbred horses from England to North America. Thereafter, it became popular practice to cross Narragansett mares with Thoroughbred stallions, which resulted in a larger, more refined all-purpose animal which became known simply as the American horse.

It is perhaps fortunate this cross-breeding was done so soon after the importation of the Thoroughbred to the Colonies, so that Narragansett blood would continue to course through the veins of American horses. The Narragansett Pacer as an American breed was short-lived. Rustic bridle paths through the woods soon became wide, well-travelled highways and, as in the rest of the settled world, carriages supplanted saddle horses as the most popular mode of transportation. The little Narragansett's claim to fame was his fast, smooth saddle gait—he was poorly suited as a carriage horse. For this reason, the sturdy little Narragansett became highly expendable.

Plantation owners in the Spanish speaking West Indies still depended upon saddle horses to help them survey their vast plantations. These men were so impressed by the Narragansett Pacer that they bought and exported them to the Caribbean Islands in large numbers. All these factors led to the breed being virtually eliminated from this country by 1820. The Narragansett's valuable pacing blood, however, was passed on through some of their

Thoroughbred progeny. It was also saved through Narragansett horses that had been sent to Canada—which horses helped to create the Standardbred pacer, a horse used for driving and harness racing. Narragansett breeding was also contributed to the Canadian Pacer, a wiry little pacing horse with ancestors originating in the courts of Louis 14th of France. Some authorities believe that the Narragansett exported to the West Indies were primary foundation stock for the Paso Fino.

THE AMERICAN HORSE

In the English Colonies the horse that was developed by crossing Narragansett and Thoroughbreds was larger and prettier than the former, but retained the easy riding gaits. This horse, the first Saddlebred type, was popular by the time of the American Revolution. The existence of the American Horse was noted in a letter from an American diplomat to France in 1776.

FOUNDATION SIRES OF THE AMERICAN SADDLEBRED

Blaze, a celebrated Thoroughbred who became the foundation sire for the Hackney, was foaled in 1733. This horse was destined to influence the American Saddlebred more than any other. It can rightfully be claimed that the Thoroughbred Blaze is the true "great grandsire" of the American Saddlebred horse.

DENMARK F.S.

In 1839 a Thoroughbred stallion, Denmark, was foaled at the Samuel Davis farm near Danville, Kentucky. Denmark was eight generations removed from Blaze. Though we have no paintings or photographs of this horse, it was said by James Farris, who exercised Denmark, that he was 16 hands high, dark brown in color, and had a "long rangy neck and gay tail." Denmark was a four-mile racing Thoroughbred, but sired many fine Saddle Horses.

In 1891, as a result of the concerted efforts of a number of Saddle Horse

Breeders, the first registry association for an American horse was formed. Charles F. Mills of Springfield, Illinois had been collecting proposed registrations and information about various Saddle Horse lines at the request of breeders from Missouri and other Midwestern states. This information piqued the interest of "Kentucky Saddler" horse breeders. John B. Castleman, of Louisville, traveled to Missouri to meet with breeders and propose a national association. On April 8, 1891, the National Saddle Horse Breeders' Association was formed in Louisville, Kentucky.

The following year saw the publication of the first registry volume, and fourteen Saddle Horse Foundation Sires were named. By 1899 that number had been increased to seventeen, and the registry's name was changed to the American Saddle Horse Breeder's Association. In 1902 the Association decreased the number of recognized foundation sires to ten. In 1908 it was determined that fully 55% of all the Saddle Horses recorded in the first volume of the stud book traced back to the Thoroughbred Denmark, and he was designated the lone Foundation Sire. At this time he became officially known as Denmark F.S. The other foundation sires were designated Sires of Note, and given regular registration numbers.

The most prepotent son of Denmark F.S. was Gaines Denmark, foaled in 1851 out of the Stevenson Mare, a natural ambling mare by Cockspur. Cockspur was a naturally gaited stallion of Thoroughbred and/or Canadian Pacer breeding. Cockspur not only sired Gaines Denmark, but his blood was contributed to many lines of fine Saddlebred horses. Gaines Denmark, a flashy black five-gaited show horse, was noted for his beauty and easy saddle gaits, as well as for a his extremely proud—one could even say vain—carriage. This quality, largely passed down through the line of Gaines Denmark, was to become a trademark of the American Saddlebred.

HARRISON CHIEF

Harrison Chief, foaled in 1872, was another horse that would be recognized as a Saddle Horse Foundation Sire—though his right to this role wasn't formally acknowledged until nearly a century following his death. Harrison Chief was not officially designated Foundation Sire until 1991, the year the American Saddlebred Horse Association celebrated its centennial. During his lifetime he was a registered Trotting Horse, though knowledgeable horsemen were aware that his get frequently possessed the saddle gaits. Like Gaines Denmark, Harrison Chief was nine generations removed from the Thoroughbred Blaze. Harrison Chief's line to Blaze also traced through Messenger, an imported Thoroughbred who was instrumental in the founding of the Standardbred breed.

Harrison Chief was a stylish blood bay who stood over sixteen hands. Though he was never raced, he became known as a classy, top performer in harness classes of his day. He was extensively shown for eight seasons, and during those years was beaten in competition only four times.

Harrison Chief stood at stud for 21 seasons at James Cromwell's Locust Grove Breeding Farm in Cynthiana, Kentucky. During his lifetime he sired over 1,000 sons and daughters. He died in 1896. It is believed his remains lay next to Gaines Denmark's, who also stood at stud, died, and was buried at that farm.

SIRES OF NOTE

The Sires of Note who contributed to the early Saddle Horse included Brinker's Dennon, Sam Booker, John Dillard, Tom Hal, Coleman's Eureka, Van Meter's Waxy, Cabell's Lexington, Copperbottom, Stump the Dealer, Texas, Prince Albert, Peter's Halcorn, Varnon's Roebuck, Davy Crockett and Pat Cleburne. Eight of these fifteen names still make an appearance on the pedigrees of modern day American Saddlebreds.

OTHER IMPORTANT EARLY STALLIONS

There were other early significant Saddle Horse stallions who weren't given any special designation, but nevertheless made important contributions to the breed. Some of these were Artist, Black Squirrel, Montrose, Rex McDonald, Chester Dare, Bourbon Chief, Forest King, McDonald Chief, Rex Peavine and Bourbon King.

THE SADDLE HORSE MARE

A mare's contribution to a breed is necessarily limited by her ability to bear only a relatively few foals during her lifetime. The show ring helps build a mare's reputation, making her foals more valuable, but also decreases the number of years she can produce foals. Nevertheless, history records a number of Saddle Horse foundation mares who became known for producing prepotent Saddle Horse sires. The Stevenson mare, dam of Gaines Denmark, was one such horse. So were Lucy Mack, The Saltram Mare, Betsey Harrison, Pekina, Lute Boyd, Daisy 2nd, Queen 48, and Annie C.

Athleticism, beauty and style, however, has never been limited to Saddlebred stallions. Some early mares' reputations were built as much in the show ring as in the breeding shed, where they competed successfully against the best horses of their day, male or female. A few such great nineteenth century show mares were Lou Chief, Emily, Miss Rex and Belle Beach.

THE SADDLE HORSE TYPE ESTABLISHED

During the nineteenth century two distinct families of Saddle Horses evolved: The Denmark family, known for their refinement, beauty and extremely fast and graceful saddle gaits; and the Chief family, known for size, boldness and power, particularly at the trot. Both Saddlebred families, however, possessed an intangible but distinct quality called "presence."

In the early part of the 20th century American Saddlebred breeders, by judiciously crossing Chief and Denmark lines, firmly established a single type of American Saddlebred.

CONTRIBUTION OF OTHER BREEDS

It should not be assumed the Narragansett Pacer and Thoroughbred were the only breeds of horses contributing to the contemporary American Saddlebred. Like most of the culture of the country from which they sprang, American Saddlebreds as they exist today resulted from the combination of innumerable influences.

THE MORGAN

The Morgan horse descends from one prepotent stallion of uncertain parentage who was foaled in 1789. Originally this horse was called Figure, but later came to be known by the name of his second owner, Justin Morgan.

Justin Morgan and his get were renowned in New England for incredible strength, substance, style and endurance—the type of animal most in demand by colonists. Therefore, it was only natural for him and his get to be used extensively by breeders, including Saddle Horse breeders. Though Morgans as a breed were not reputed to possess the saddle gaits, some of the early Morgan horses almost certainly did, as Justin Morgan and his sons were often bred to native mares, or Narragansett Pacers, and Figure himself may have had Narragansett blood flowing in his veins.

One Morgan sire having tremendous influence on a great many other American horse breeds was Black Hawk, by Sherman Morgan, by Justin Morgan. Black Hawk was the grandsire of G.S. Rattler, who sired Peavine, an extremely influential American Saddlebred sire. Another of Black Hawk's grandsons was Indian Chief, a horse who beat the harness racing record of Dexter, a son of Hambletonian 10, the great Standardbred sire. And lest we still underestimate the importance of the Morgan horse Black Hawk to American horse breeding, it should be noted that Maggie Marshall, the dam of Allan F-1, the foundation sire for the Tennessee Walking Horse, also boasts Black Hawk as her grandsire.

CANADIAN PACERS

Canadian Pacers, closely related to the Narragansett Pacer but with distinct differences, also contributed to the development of the American Saddlebred. Three such horses are especially worth noting, as they were numbered among the original foundation sires: Tom Hal, Copperbottom and Davy Crockett. Tom Hal was foaled in 1802, and stood in Kentucky until his death in 1843. An important horse by Tom Hal was Bald Stockings, the first horse ever known to perform the running walk. Copperbottom was imported around 1812, and Davy Crockett in the 1830's. Old Pilot was yet another Canadian Pacer who "nicked well" with the early American Saddle Horses, though he was never designated a foundation sire.

OTHER BREED INFLUENCES

Blood of the Hackney horse, or England's Norfolk Trotter, was also infused into the American Saddlebred. One particular line of Thoroughbreds

HEAVENLY GAITS

tracing to the Godolphin Barb became known as Highlanders. Highlanders, particularly Highlander mares, made valuable contributions to the development of the American Saddlebred.

EARLY HORSE SHOWS

During the early 1800's horses were used primarily for power and as a means of transportation. Americans valued horses that could pull a plow all week, prance haughtily in front of the family's carriage on Sunday, and be ridden comfortably astride whenever the master of the farm (or plantation) needed to travel long distances to survey his land or visit neighbors.

Just as people take pride in their vehicles of transportation today, people of that era sought after beauty and style in their horses. The ideal horse was versatile, strong, possessed great endurance, comfortable saddle gaits, and was beautiful and stylish enough to make other men envious. Such a horse brought great prestige to its owner.

But there were few opportunities to show off a prized horse. Much of the population of young America was spread out over vast areas of land, and the hard-working caretakers of this land could ill afford to travel the long distances to town very often. County fairs helped to give these people a forum for showing their horses. These social occasions became prime opportunities for buying, selling—and merely showing off—horses. Before long the show part of this pastime became the prime consideration, and was reason enough in itself for people to travel great distances to congregate.

Though undoubtedly horse shows were common affairs previous to 1816, this was the year the first horse show was recorded in Lexington, Kentucky, an area noted for its "Kentucky Saddlers." Missouri—particularly Mexico, Missouri—was another area noted for its excellent saddle stock. The first Missouri show on record was in 1833, in conjunction with the Boone County fair.

By the mid-1800's stock men and trainers were willing to traverse great distances to bring their Saddle Horses to the show rings. Some rode the horses cross-country, some shipped them by rail, and some came by steamboat. The St. Louis Fair, established in 1856, was considered the first national horse show.

Once arrived at the site of a show, owners and/or trainers competed their animals against the best horses in the country. These occasions created a tremendous amount of excitement and anticipation in mid-nineteenth century America. The thrill of good horseflesh was not limited to horsemen, but ran along the collective spine of the general population. During this pre-movie, radio and television era, certain horses—and the people associated with them—became the nation's celebrities. A great deal of discussion and debate centered around the outcome of important upcoming shows.

But horse shows served more than vanity. Horse trainers and breeders (the "car salesmen" of the day) who consistently placed well at these shows could count on a good market for their wares. An entire industry was being built on the back of the early Saddle Horses.

Reputations in that industry were made in America's horse show rings. For this reason breeders went to great lengths to improve their stock. They began to maintain precise breeding records and to keep track of the progress of the horses produced and sold. They paid close attention to which lines of horses crossed well, and which lines and crosses were best suited for various purposes.

The Saddlebred type of horse consistently placed well in horse show competition. Their show classes were usually broken down into three categories. There were the harness horses, Saddle Horses (today's five-gaited horse) and the walk, trot and canter horses (today's three-gaited horses). While fine harness and three-gaited show horses demonstrated their abilities at the walk, trot and canter, five-gaited show horses had to perform the walk and canter, as well as a working gait, rack and slow gait. At that time the working gait might be the trot, running walk, fox trot or single-foot, while the slow gait was either the fox trot or stepping pace. Some of these horses performed such a wide spectrum of easy gaits that they never resorted to the trot in the show ring.

Certain lines of Saddle Horses were valued for their ability to perform the easy saddle gaits. Though most show horses had to be taught how to perform the rack and stepping pace, or at least how to perform them with the correct show horse style, not all horses possessed the innate ability to learn. Some Saddle Horses were born natural gaited and required little more than some professional polish to prepare for the show ring. Other horses were very difficult to gait—but could do a blazing rack or extremely slow and stylish slow

HEAVENLY GAITS

gait, once they caught on to what was expected of them.

Throughout the Saddlebred's early history, there have been horses renowned for their saddle gaits. Gaines Denmark was one such horse, and it is reputed that during his extensive show career in the 1850's, he remained unbeaten as a five-gaited show horse. During this time in the south, trotting horses were so little esteemed that horse show rules didn't require the horses to show at the trot, though the early registry required all show horses to be examined and certified as being able to perform at least two of the saddle gaits. Not until 1888, when a larger number of Easterners began to participate in horse shows, were the rules modified to require all show horses to demonstrate the trot. Around this time there was an infusion of harness horse blood introduced into gaited saddle horse lines.

FAMOUS WAR HORSES

The Civil War (1861-1865) interrupted the major horse shows, but horses who were the forebears of today's Saddlebred continued to build legendary reputations even during the war. Many Saddle Horses spent the war years serving as mounts for Civil War generals. Two Thoroughbred sires' names that frequently appear on Saddlebred pedigrees were Grey Eagle and Lexington. General E. Lee's famous horse Traveller was by Grey Eagle. Traveller became nearly as famous as the General, himself. The Thoroughbred racehorse Lexington sired General Sherman's horse (also named Lexington), General U.S. Grant's two horses, Charger and Cincinnati. General George Meade rode Baldy, a gaited saddle horse, while the smooth saddle gaits of Little Sorrell carried Stonewall Jackson through the war. The Confederate commands of Generals John Hunt Morgan and Nathan Bedford Forrest were mounted almost exclusively on American Saddle Horses—these horses became known for great feats of endurance during the war.

Horses were perhaps the most important element of unification between the North and South at the end of the war when the victorious General Grant allowed the defeated Confederate soldiers to keep their horses at the surrender of Appomattox. Other Union Commanders followed suit. Since the economic prosperity of Southerners depended more than ever upon the "Kentucky Saddler," this act was a decisive factor in south's ability to rebound economically after the war.

ANOTHER SHOW RING HEYDAY

Following the war, horsemen returned to the show rings of America in droves. Besides the already established shows in Kentucky, Virginia and Missouri, large, prominent horse shows were organized in the eastern and Midwesterner parts of the country. This was the Saddle Horse's hey-day, a time when the reputations of certain horses, and the horsemen associated with them, took on mythical proportions. Great horses and the people associated with them served as celebrities and heroes for a war-weary, but still vital, young nation.

Montrose, a five-gaited horse foaled in 1869, was America's first post-war superstar show horse. Herbert Krum wrote:

> *After much hoopla to clear a path through adoring crowds, Montrose would enter the ring at a full gallop, making one or two rounds before he settled down to work. During a show career of 14 years he defeated every horse shown against him. Montrose was sold 12 times and was the first Saddle Horse to command $5,000. He was champion at the St. Louis Fair, considered the leading show in America, at age 17.*

Montrose stock, however, earned a reputation for being wildly temperamental and hard to train. A common caution among horsemen was "A Montrose will kill you." Still, Montrose's fine attributes and show record placed him much in demand as a sire—bookings to the popular stallion had to be arranged a year or more ahead of time. Not everyone desiring his services had the patience, or time, to wait that long. This set of circumstances was at least partially responsible for the creation of Montrose's successor to the title "show ring superstar."

A Saddle Horse breeder from Missouri named Joe McDonald planned to breed one of his best mares, Lucy Mack, to Montrose. The elderly McDonald was suffering from very poor health, however, and decided that if he wanted to see the results of Lucy Mack's next breeding, he could ill afford to wait for a booking to the great Montrose. And so he arranged to breed Lucy

Mack with Rex Denmark, another extremely popular and talented 5-gaited show horse of that era. In the show ring Rex Denmark exhibited great masculinity and presence, the epitome of power. Montrose boasted speed, a long, graceful swan-like neck, and finely chiseled features. His was the epitome of refined equine beauty.

Lucy Mack was bred to Rex Denmark, and the ungainly black foal she dropped in 1890 as a result of that union appeared so unpromising at first that the Harrison family, who owned both Rex Denmark and Montrose, gave Joe McDonald's Lucy Mack a complimentary breeding to Star Rose, Montrose's best son.

But Rex McDonald, the ugly little foal by Rex Denmark and out of Lucy Mack, was to prove that not even the best and most experienced horse breeders are always right about judging the potential of newborn foals. Rex McDonald grew up to become the greatest and most popular show horse the world had ever known.

Rex McDonald possessed the beautiful head that was the characteristic trademark of the Denmark line of Saddle Horses. This was combined with a body inhabited by power, grace and speed. He was sweet-tempered, took easily to training, and could be ridden with good results by horsemen at every level of ability. Perhaps Rex McDonald's most outstanding feature was the way he moved under saddle. His was such a poetry of locomotion, beauty, power and pure saddle gaits, that he proved nearly invincible in the show ring. His presence overwhelmed the competition, and cast a giant shadow over the horse show rings of America, and especially over the rest of the Saddle Horse world.

In the year 1900, when Rex McDonald was ten years old, he was considered invincible in the show ring. It has been reported that at that time Saddle Horse breeders got together and drew up a petition to force his owner to retire him from competition. According to this account he was officially declared unbeatable, and was to be shown only in exhibition, rather than in competition. It seems more likely, however, that shows simply could not get entries if Rex McDonald competed, so show officials requested that Rex put on special exhibitions in lieu of showing. This is what he did in that year.

Rex McDonald began competing again the following show season, however. In October of 1903 Rex McDonald was declared Grand Champion

Rex McDonald performing the slow gait. The famous show horse was at an advanced age when this photo was shot.

horse at the last St. Louis Horse Fair ever held. Shortly thereafter he was retired for good. Rex McDonald was thirteen years old, a ten-year veteran of the show circuit, and in over one thousand competitions had been defeated only six times.

One defeat in 1897 came at the hands of a man accustomed to breaking with tradition: He was beaten by Tom Bass, riding a Saddle Horse mare named Miss Rex. Tom Bass was not only a celebrated horseman, but a black man who played an important role in raising the collective social consciousness of a nation.

TOM BASS

Tom Bass was born into slavery, the son of his white master William Bass and a black slave woman, Cornelia Gray. But an incredible talent with horses, combined with an easy-going, winning personality and an enterprising spirit enabled him to surmount many of the racial barriers that faced blacks in America during his lifetime (1859-1934). Tom Bass worked hard and tenaciously, and became not only the first black man allowed in America's horse show rings, but one of the most respected men of his era.

Miss Rex was a Saddle Horse mare trained and ridden by Tom Bass. He taught her to perform both as a five-gaited show horse, and for High School classes. High School classes were the equivalent of today's Grand Prix dressage, with solo horse and rider teams performing complicated ballet-like maneuvers, often set to music. Before training Miss Rex, Tom Bass had become known for training Columbus, a celebrated High School gelding Bass had actually taught to canter backwards. (This was a maneuver he was reputed to have first taught to a cantankerous, cast-off mule when he was just eight years old). Columbus went on to become "Buffalo" Bill Cody's most celebrated trick horse.

In contrast to Columbus' masculinity, Miss Rex was small and dainty but, as Tom Bass liked to declare, she "was bold and had a loud way of going." In 1896 the two were such a popular item that it was reported that Queen Victoria of England requested a command performance—a request that the sea-wary Tom Bass turned down, with regrets.

There were few other opportunities that Tom Bass and his equine pupils missed in his lifetime. During an era when black men and women in America labored under the shameful yoke of discrimination, this unassuming black horseman was making a many contributions, not only to a special breed of horse, but to history.

Unhappy with bits he considered to be inhumane to his charges, Tom Bass was credited with popularizing a curb bit which became known as the Bass Bit. This bit came into widespread use, and is still employed today.

Though his hometown during most of his adult life was in Mexico, Missouri, for a time he operated a stable in Kansas City, Missouri. In 1893, when the Kansas City Fire Department needed to earn money, Bass suggested a horse show which was the forerunner of the Royal. This became a prestigious American horse show that is still being held today.

Though he owned only a few of the horses he became renowned for working with, Tom Bass bred, raised, trained and rode many of the most celebrated horses of his day. This list includes Forest King, Columbus, Miss Rex, Frances McDonald, Rex Blees, Belle Beach, Highland Squirrel King, Chester Peavine, and many, many others.

According to one account Chester Dare, an extremely important Saddle Horse sire, owed his life and career to Tom Bass. As a young horse he was accidentally blinded in one eye, and became impossible to handle. His owners, after consulting with several knowledgeable horsemen, reluctantly concluded that the fine stallion would have to be destroyed.

Bass historian Bill Downey recounts how Colonel Graves, the stallion's owner, called Bass as a last resort. Bass believed the magnificent Chester Dare could be saved, and requested the chance to work with him. Though the horse was considered to be too dangerous to handle, Bass concluded that the horse was simply frustrated by being half-blind. So, with his customary tact, Bass by himself somehow found a way to blindfold the defensive stallion. Unable to see a thing, the horse learned to trust the trainer's gentle voice and, eventually, the guidance of his skillful seat, legs and hands. Thanks to his patient perseverance, Chester Dare went on to become a celebrated show horse and sired hundreds of outstanding Saddle Horses. The favor was returned as, according to Downey, Chester Dare was Bass' first significant foray into the "white man's" realm of horses.

Bass was the first black man to show in many of the country's most prominent horse shows. He regularly faced the cruel wounds of discrimination, being forced to travel in Negro sections of trains and eat only in Negro restaurants. Though many blacks and a few liberal whites accused Bass of being a self-effacing "Uncle Tom" with too little concern for the cause of his race, Bass' accomplishments as a man undoubtedly helped many prejudiced people to begin seeing past the color of a man's skin. This was certainly an important step toward racial equality.

Tom Bass evoked great loyalty from his friends—and he had many friends. Once, at the Iowa State Fair in Des Moines, he was prohibited from showing his horses because of his race. When news of this episode spread, Saddle Horse breeders, religious leaders, leading political figures, well-known writers and the general population became so incensed that by the next year the Iowa State Fair Board of Directors had been replaced. The new board members afforded Tom Bass red carpet treatment at the Iowa State Fair Horse Show the following year. On that occasion Tom Bass literally stole the show. When the competitions were over, Bass had garnered the greatest sweep of victories in the history of the show. His quiet revenge was surely sweet—and complete. Even the American Cup Event, which was for Iowa horses only, was won by a horse that had been purchased the previous year by Ralph C. Hamilton of Iowa—from Missouri's Tom Bass.

During his lifetime the nation's most respected horsemen—Joseph Potts, John T. Hughes, John Hook, Buffalo Bill Cody, Ben Glenn, and Alfred

HEAVENLY GAITS

Vanderbilt, among others—were friends and admirers of Tom Bass. This popularity extended outside the horse world. This son of a slave woman counted Presidents Calvin Coolidge, Grover Cleveland, William McKinley, William H. Taft and Theodore Roosevelt among his personal friends.

Overcoming serious physical problems caused by a horse show mishap, as well as prejudice, Tom Bass's horse show career spanned the period of history covering the early development and promotion of the American Saddlebred horse. He trained and showed horses until he was seventy years old. Near the end of his career, a New York city newspaper paper declared: "An American Phenomenon, Tom Bass is America's greatest individual horseman."

Upon hearing of the death of Tom Bass, in 1934, his friend and syndicated columnist Will Rogers wrote the following:

> *"Tom Bass, well known Negro horseman, aged 75, died in Mexico, Missouri today. . . You have all seen society folks perhaps on beautiful three or five gaited Saddle Horses and said: 'My what skill and patience they must have had to train that animal.'*
>
> *"Well, all they did was ride him. All this Negro, Tom Bass did was train him. For over 50 years America's premier horse trainer. He trained thousands that others were applauded on. A remarkable man. A remarkable character. . .If old Saint Peter is as wise as we give him credit for being, Tom, he will let you go in on horseback and give those folks up there a great show, and you'll get the blue ribbons yourself."*

Whether or not Mr. Bass is still receiving blue ribbons in heaven, his legacy to the American Saddlebred is well worth remembering, and recounting here.

NEW ERA, NEW BLOOD

As the twentieth century dawned, the automobile began superseding the horse as a means of transportation. Devoted Saddle Horse people,

George Ford Morris painting of Bourbon King, foaled in 1900. Bourbon King was the great progenitor of the Chief family of American Saddlebreds. (Courtesy ASHA).

however, continued to compete with their horses in America's show rings, and individual horses continued to catch the admiration and imagination of a nation.

The first year of the new century saw the birth of another extraordinarily prepotent American Saddlebred sire. Bourbon King, by Bourbon Chief, by Harrison Chief F.S., was foaled in 1900. Bourbon King's dam was Annie C, who also traced back to Harrison Chief F.S. through her sire, Wilson's King.

Not only was Bourbon King an outstanding horse in his own right, but his prepotency as a stallion was such that the Harrison Chief F.S. line of Saddlebreds traces to Harrison F.S. through Bourbon King. Though foaled nearly fifty years after the birth of Gaines Denmark (1851), Bourbon King was to be to the Harrison Chief F.S. line of American Saddlebreds what Gaines Denmark was to the Denmark F.S. line. It is interesting to note that this horse was purchased as a weanling from Mat Cohen by Allie G. Jones for the stupendous sum of $125.

Though horse shows continued to be popular entertainment, the first quarter of the twentieth century was a relatively uneventful period for the American Saddle Horse world. No single horse managed to catch and fire the nation's imagination the way Rex McDonald had. But during this time, when little was happening on the surface, horsemen continued to uphold the American Saddle Horse's tradition of excellence.

THEY MADE THEIR MARK

Literally dozens of large farms were dedicated to producing top quality American Saddle Horses during the early part of this century. John Hook was a famous horseman who fairly represents others of his era. He was instrumental in the founding of two of the nation's largest and most reputable Saddle Horse operations. In 1913 Hook, who at the time owned a training stable with John Woods, was recruited by R.A. Long of Lee's Summit, Missouri, to manage his stable at Longview Farms. Under Hook, Longview became one of the best sources of excellent Saddle Horse stock in the country. Many show ring wonders were produced under its banner.

In 1925 Hook was hired away from Longview by E.A. Stuart, owner of the Carnation Milk Company. Stuart commissioned Hook to design and oversee a stable near Los Angeles, California. The Carnation Stables, built during the height of the depression, cost in excess of $70,000, and housed 60 to 70 horses. The appointments of this stable were so luxurious that, when its grand opening was held, nearly 8,000 people attended.

John Hook, like many of the celebrated horsemen of his day, was more than a good stable manager. He trained and rode such horses as Grand McDonald, Easter Cloud, Rex Blees, My Major Dare and The Gingerbread Man.

The stallions Rex Peavine and Bourbon King were making their contributions during this time. These two horses sired so many five-gaited World's Champions that their names are indelibly marked in the history of the American Saddlebred horse.

Rex Peavine was a prepotent five-gaited American Saddle Horse sire who was named 1903 five-gaited World's Champion at St. Louis in 1903. He sired Edna May, a celebrated Saddle Horse show mare who was the five-gaited American Saddle Horse World's Champion in 1909. Edna May in turn produced Edna May's King (by Bourbon King), who won the five-gaited World's Championship in 1924 and 1926. Other five-gaited World's Champion Saddle Horses sired by Rex Peavine include Hazel Dawn, (1912 and 1913); Liberty Girl (1919); Mass of Gold (1920, 1921, 1923); and Dark Rex (1927).

Bourbon King, who took the five-gaited World's Championship in

1905, also sired five-gaited World Champions. Among these were Astral King (1915), Richlieu King (1916), and Edna May's King (1924, 1926).

A few American Saddle Horses reigned supreme as five-gaited champions during the late nineteen-twenties, thirties and forties. Among those not already named who won the five-gaited World's Championship more than once during these years were Chief of Longview (1928, 1929), Sweetheart On Parade (1931, 1932), Belle Le Rose (1933, 1934), A Sensation (1940, 1941), and Oak Hill Chief (1943, 1945, 1946).

Anacacho Denmark, a son of Edna May's King, was foaled in 1930. He was to become the leading sire of five-gaited champion American Saddle Horses, and was the only horse ever to sire all of the five-gaited divisional winners and grand champions at the World's Championship Horse Show.

WING COMMANDER

In 1946 a three-year-old dark chestnut stallion named Wing Commander charged into the nation's show scene and swept away all the competition. Wing Commander lived up to the superstar tradition established by Rex McDonald in the 1800's. Wing Commander not only won the title of five-gaited World's Champion six years running (1948-1953), but was shown in most of the major shows for nine years, to be defeated only twice, in 1947, as a four-year old. Both times the young stallion was beaten by Daneshell's Easter Parade, the beautiful but erratic five-gaited World's Champion of 1947.

Wing Commander was owned by Dodge Stables, and trained and shown by the stable's well-known horse trainer, Earl Teater. He was a dark chestnut horse, with four socks, a neat stripe, and some flax in his mane and tail. Wing Commander possessed powerful gaits—though teaching this horse with the unbelievable hock action to rack was a real challenge for Mr. Teater. Once the eager-to-please young stallion caught on to what was expected of him, however, he performed the gait with incredible speed, consistency, and precision.

Wing Commander won 167 tough competitions and nearly $50,000 during his nine-year career. He retired to stud in 1954, and died of colic in

1969, at the age of 26 years.

Wing Commander's abilities were carried on through his progeny. Besides three-gaited and fine harness horses, Wing Commander sired two five-gaited World's Champions, and was grandsire of another. The first of these was Valerie Emerald (1969). The next outstanding five-gaited show ring celebrity by Wing Commander was Yorktown, who held the World's Champion title in 1970, 1971 and 1972. Sky Watch, Wing Commander's grandson, was World's Champion four times. Sky Watch won the title as a young horse in 1982, 1983 and 1984, then staged a dramatic comeback in 1988 when he earned the five-gaited World's Championship once more.

Following Wing Commander's retirement other talented Saddlebred horses were finally able to win the World's Championship shows in Lexington. Lady Carrigan was the five-gaited World's Champion for four years (1954, 1955, 1957, 1958). Plainview's Julia (1959, 1960) and Denmark's Daydream (1961, 1962) each held the title twice. Some people believe that the lovely Daydream's untimely death was the only thing that prevented her from becoming an equine superstar on the order of Rex McDonald or Wing Commander.

CH Wing Commander, Earl Teater up.

Photo by John R. Horst; Courtesy ASHA

DENMARK'S DAYDREAM

The story of Denmark's Daydream illustrates the ecstacy, and the heartache, common to people who dedicate their lives to creating great show horses. Daydream was aptly named. She was a brilliant light chestnut, with flaxen mane and tail. The dainty mare possessed an ethereal beauty, and moved as though her delicate feet were borne upon the fleece of a cloud. Sired by the Oman Stable's incomparable Anacacho Denmark, Daydream's life began more like a nightmare. She demonstrated unmistakable signs of greatness right from the first, but her owner, Doss Stanton, wondered if her difficult-to-handle temperament would prevent her from becoming a top-ranking show horse. This seemed a moot point, however, when the three-year old Daydream seriously injured her right front foot, catching it in her stall door and pulling it loose around the coronet band. Even after healing began, it appeared she would never be sound enough to show, so Daydream was removed from training to become a broodmare. In 1958, at five years of age, she dropped her only foal, Oman's Sir Echo, later to become famous as 21 Guns.

CH Denmark's Daydream with trainer Lee Roby aboard.

Photo by Sargent

HEAVENLY GAITS

Daydream's foot did heal thoroughly, however, and motherhood had the added benefit of settling the mare's temperament. A more tractable Daydream (who was never shown under her full name) was placed back in gaited training for the show ring. Lee Roby, the trainer for Greenhill Stables in Tulsa, Oklahoma, spotted her being worked on the grounds of the Kentucky State fair, in 1958. Roby was so impressed by the gorgeous Daydream that he immediately bought her for Mrs. J.R. Sharp, the owner of Greenhill Stables.

Daydream possessed stamina, beautiful gaits, presence, and near-perfect conformation. In 1961 this matron brood mare attained the reputation of being virtually unbeatable in the nation's top show rings. Lee Roby considered her to be the best horse he had ever trained—and he had trained a number of the top American Saddle Horse show ring contenders of the day, including the two-time five-gaited World Champion Oakhill's Chief (1945,1946).

But Daydream's career was tragically shortened by a virus that decimated the American horse world in 1963. Early in the 1963 show season, still in her prime at ten years of age, Denmark's Daydream took ill. Though at first she seemed to have won a victory over the deadly virus, she soon suffered a second bout, and was too weak to beat it. The great competitor, Denmark's Daydream, had lost her most important battle.

The one foal by Daydream, 21 Guns, had also been purchased from Oman Stables by Mrs. Sharp's Greenhill Stables. This fine horse lived up to his dam's promise by winning both a championship and a reserve grand championship at the American Royal Horse Show in 1964. Unfortunately, 21 Guns was a gelding.

MY-MY

Daydream's untimely death cast a pall over the nation's 1963 American Saddlebred show rings. Only a very special horse could take her place in the hearts of America's horse people. Fortunately just such a horse, My-My, a daughter of the five-gaited World's Champion Daneshell's Easter Parade—the only horse ever to beat Wing Commander—was waiting her chance. My-My, like her dam, was trained and shown by Frank Bradshaw.

My-My was a bright copper chestnut. Though her gaits and action were

CH MY MY, six times winner of World's Grand Championship 5-Gaited Division at the Kentucky State Fair. Ridden by Frank Bradshaw.

remarkably similar to her dam's, her conformation was much less refined. Jolie Richardson owned the mare from 1964 on, and described the three-year old My-My as "gawky and awkward," with a too-large head and massive shoulder. To make matters worse the mare—also like her dam—was extremely temperamental. Frank Bradshaw was the only man ever able to ride her.

But the gawky and awkward, hard to handle My-My grew into her noble features. Her size and powerful conformation gave her incredible stamina while enabling her to perform her gaits like a perfectly synchronized, powerful driving machine—a living, breathing machine who, under the tactful guidance of Frank Bradshaw would roll right over the competition.

After paying her show ring dues in 1961 and 1962 My-My did just that. Starting in 1963, she was shown undefeated. She not only earned the 1963 World's Championship, but won the hearts of spectators all over the country. My-My maintained the title of World's Champion for six consecutive years (1963-1968), being the only five-gaited horse to match Wing Commander's six-time World's Championship record. Had she lived, she might even have

51

gone on to beat Wing Commander's record. Once again, however, a celebrated mare's career was cut short by tragic circumstances. My-My died of a suspected brain tumor in 1969.

THE BRADSHAW BROTHERS

Many outstanding individuals made important contributions to the American Saddlebred world—and a love for these horses seems to run particularly strong in some families. Garland and Frank Bradshaw, brothers from Lebanon, Tennessee, are a case in point. Both men worked at Longview Farms in Lee's Summit, Missouri, but each went on to become an extraordinary horse trainer in his own right.

Garland Bradshaw, the older of the two brothers, was known for producing some of the most exciting horses in the Saddle Horse world, including five-gaited World Champions Lady Jane and Lady Carrigan. Garland preferred to start with natural gaited animals, those who demonstrated a natural rack or ambling gait. Though most five-gaited trainers eschew these horses because they can be difficult to teach to trot, Garland believed that a natural ability to gait gave a horse more exciting high leg action once it did learn the trot, and therefore contributed to its show ring persona.

At least one horse helped to prove Garland's theory. The Lemon Drop Kid, who was Fine Harness World's Champion for four years (1956-1959), became so popular as an exciting trotting fine harness horse that his photo appeared on the cover of *Sports Illustrated*. Yet The Lemon Drop Kid was so strongly gaited that he was written off by his breeders as strictly a pacing/racking horse until he reached the age of two years!

Garland Bradshaw's brother Frank rode the incomparable My-My to her six five-gaited World's Championships, and then followed that amazing feat with a win for the title on Valerie Emerald in 1969. Frank Bradshaw was the only trainer to ever earn the coveted five-gaited world title seven consecutive years.

THE TEATER BROTHERS, AND OTHERS

Two other famous Saddle Horse trainer brothers were Earl and Lloyd Teater. Lloyd Teater rode Belle Le Rose (1933, 1934) and A Sensation (1940, 1941) to five-gaited World Championships. Just a few years later his brother Earl guided Wing Commander to his incomparable record of wins.

Not all relatives who are well known Saddlebred promoters are siblings. Mr. and Mrs. Hugh Richardson and their daughter, Jolie, were all closely involved with top-notch Saddlebreds, as is the trainer Redd Crabtree and his parents, Charles and Helen Crabtree. Helen Crabtree has enjoyed many victories from the back of American Saddlebreds; one she is particularly proud of is that of being the last rider (on the world's amateur five-gaited World Champion, Legal Tender, (in 1962) to win in competition against My-My.

"I'm the last one to beat My-My," Ms. Crabtree told Billy Reed of *The Louisville Courier Journal* in 1974, "but I have to keep quiet about it because all the men will get mad!"

WOMEN OF NOTE

Though the world of horses has historically been dominated by men, many women have been intimately involved in promoting the American Saddlebred. Numbered among these were women such as Mrs. W.P. Roth, who owned Chief of Longview and Sweetheart on Parade; Mrs. J.R. Sharp, who owned Greenhill Stables; Mrs. R.C. Tway, owner of Plainview farms; Frances Dodge Van Lennep, mistress of the famed Dodge Stables; and Jolie Richardson, who owned five-gaited World's Champions Lady Carrigan and My-My, among other great horses.

Michelle MacFarlane is a woman with an enviable show ring record. Ms. MacFarlane engineered the 1988 five-gaited World's Championship comeback of the eleven-year-old Sky Watch. This dedicated horsewoman was not only the first woman to ever take the coveted title, but was only the second amateur rider to ever take the blue in the history of the World's Championship.

Trainer Tom Moore possesses the distinction of having won the greatest number of Saddlebred World's Championships overall. He is also the only rider ever to have entered, and won, in every division of the Kentucky State Fair in Louisville, Kentucky.

Before closing this all-too-brief highlight of famous Saddlebred people, we will mention the accomplished Don Harris. Harris promoted the magnificent Imperator to his four five-gaited World's Championship titles (1980, 1981, 1985, 1986).

Throughout this breed's history there have been many outstanding personalities who devoted their lives to breeding, training and promoting excellence in the American Saddlebred. Though it is impossible to name them all, their legacies live on in the flesh of the beautiful horse they helped to create.

CH Yorktown, son of Rex McDonald, held the World's Champion title in 1971, 1972 and 1973. Tom Moore is up.

Photo by Sargent

Don Harris on CH Imperator, the horse he rode to four five-gaited World Championships (1980, 1981, 1985 & 1986)

OTHER USES FOR THE AMERICAN SADDLEBRED

The account thus far may give the impression that, aside from a few years during the Civil War, American Saddlebred horses have been good for little more than show. Though they were and are extraordinary show horses, they are also one of the most versatile of horses. This is to be expected since Saddlebreds have been continuously bred for power and tractability, as well as for beauty and style. This breed of horse had to meet the exacting demands of people whose goals were to produce horses that would serve as a standard against which all other breeds could be measured.

Since this book is about gaited horses and riding, we will only make passing reference to the many ways in which the non-gaited American Saddlebred is used: dressage; western pleasure; country pleasure; hunter-jumper; gymkhana events; roping; cutting; reining; parading. The Saddlebred makes an extremely powerful and stylish sleigh or carriage horse—and has plowed its share of fields and skidded more than a few logs, as well!

American Saddlebreds, naturally gaited or otherwise, serve as pleasure and trail horses, on mounted police forces, and as hardy, sure-footed mounts for forest rangers in our national forests. Regardless of the use to which they are put, these horses usually excel, and are delightful coworkers and companions.

EQUINE MOVIE STARS

It should be no surprise considering the breed's intelligence, beauty, responsiveness and personality that some American Saddlebreds have been famous T.V. and/or film entertainers, or were owned by such. Arthur Godfrey's "Goldie" was an American Saddlebred, as was television's wily but lovable talking horse, "Mr. Ed."

The contemporary actor William Shatner is deeply involved with the American Saddlebred, and owns Belle Reve Farm in Kentucky. Mr. Shatner lends his name and sponsorship to a special class for Saddlebreds shown western style.

Black Beauty and Fury, two of the most well-recognized equine movie stars, were actually one horse. Both roles, and many others, were played by a black Saddlebred stallion with the real-life moniker of Highland Dale—though his trainer Ralph McCutcheon always called him "Beauts." It's little wonder Highland Dale aka: Beauts, Black Beauty, Fury possessed such charisma and took so easily to training: the personality stallion boasted the blue-blood of such notables as Rex Peavine, Forest King, Thornton's Star, and Rex Denmark. Highland Dale earned over half-a-million dollars over his show career, and was the second highest paid animal in Hollywood (after Lassie).

A five-gaited black Saddlebred named Black Diamond was cast in Walt Disney's movie *Zorro!*, as well as in a number of other films. The famous movie horse trainer Les Hilton said that Black Diamond was the most versatile actor he'd ever worked with, and was game to do any trick without benefit of a double.

SPEAKING OF TRICKS. . .

A black Saddlebred horse foaled in 1921 probably deserves recognition as being the most unique equine entertainer of all time—and probably the smoothest going, as well. A curious, enterprising man named Hugh E. Winkler from Newman, Illinois, obtained this horse, who was the last registered son of Rex Peavine. In an effort to earn money during the depression, Winkler trained the stallion to roller skate. Yes, roller skate. The horse was named, aptly enough, Two-Step.

PHYSICAL CHARACTERISTICS OF THE SADDLEBRED

Many people believe that the American Saddlebred is the world's most beautiful horse. Though beauty is largely a subjective consideration—being as it is "in the eye of the beholder"—the conformation and proportions of this breed offer substantive objective evidence to back up such claims.

The Saddlebred stands between 15 and 17 hands high at the withers, with 15.3 being the average height. He comes in a full spectrum of colors, including bay, chestnut, brown, black and grey, with chestnut being the most common color. The Saddlebred may exhibit these colors in varying shades of roan. The American Saddlebred Horse Association also registers palomino and spotted Saddlebreds.

The head of the Saddlebred is very refined. His ears are small and usually demonstrate an attractive hook at the tips; the eye is large, well-rounded, and extremely expressive; his muzzle straight, and the throat latch clean. His head sets high into a medium-to-long length neck that is beautifully flexed at the poll. There is a distinctive, graceful arch all along the upper neckline.

The Saddlebred's wither is high and well-defined, and the top line of the neck sets smoothly into it. His back is level and short, with strong coupling to the hip and loins. The Saddlebred's tail is attached high to a croup that sets slightly lower than the withers. Though flat "table top" croups have long been the show ring style, it has now become recognized that a deeper slant to the croup is more likely to produce a strong 5-gaited horse. The Saddlebred's loins are amply, but smoothly, muscled; his ribs well-sprung, but shallow.

HEAVENLY GAITS

Likewise he has a substantial, yet smoothly muscled chest. The Saddlebred's body, though extremely powerful, is in no way rough or coarse in appearance.

The legs of a Saddlebred should exhibit substantial bone, and smooth muscling to the knees and hocks. They should be straight, with large, well-defined joints. This horse possesses a naturally proud stance, and is often exhibited in a slightly stretched manner. This, however, is strictly a matter of style—the horse's legs should naturally set under his body, so that a line drawn vertically from the point of buttock to the ground will run straight down the back edge of the hind leg, when the cannon is in a vertical position to the ground. The Saddlebred's comfortable, springy riding gaits can be attributed to a deep, laid back shoulder and generally long, sloping pasterns. His foot is neat, well-shaped, and of a size appropriate to the individual.

TACK FOR THE SADDLEBRED

The Saddlebred can be ridden in any style of tack appropriate to the way the animal is being used, be it dressage, western pleasure, hunter-jumper; parade or costume classes. The five-gaited show horse, however, is always shown in a flat english style (saddleseat) saddle, with a double bridle. This kind of lightweight saddle frees the horse's shoulder, enabling him to perform with very high front leg action. The double bridle carries a jointed snaffle bit, used to collect and guide the horse, and a curb bit, used to set the horse's head. The double bridle has four reins, with one set of reins attached to each bit. Thus, this style of riding requires some finesse.

In addition to the saddle and bridle, tradition dictates that show horses have set tails. This requires that the horse wears a tail set which consists of a light harness and crupper. A minor surgical procedure is performed so the horse can comfortably wear this device. Handlers and grooms must be painstaking in their care of horses with set tail devices.

The Saddlebred performs with such long strides that there is always the possibility of his overreaching with his hind foot, to strike and injure a front foot. For this reason, most Saddlebreds show with protective quarter boots on their front feet.

USUAL HANDLING & TRAINING METHODS

Though spirited, Saddlebreds are generally very responsive to people and if handled with tact take eagerly to training. It is not this work's purpose to teach anyone how to become a horse trainer, but a general outline of the steps usually taken with the horse will help the reader to better understand the animal's psyche.

Usually the Saddlebred foal is handled from a very early age in order to accustom him to close association with people. It may be taught to lead when only a few weeks old; once learned, this lesson is followed by teaching it to tie. Somewhere between the ages of four and seven months, the foal is weaned, at which time it becomes a "weanling," rather than a "foal."

Weanlings and yearlings (horses are considered to be yearlings from January 1st of their second year) are generally left alone, except perhaps for regular grooming routines, until they reach the age of about eighteen months, when work on the longe line may be started. Longeing teaches the young horse to respect and respond to the handler's body and voice aids. Plus, the exercise muscles up the animal in preparation for work under harness and/or saddle.

Most trainers teach young Saddlebreds to drive with a light cart before they are asked to accept a rider. This is an ideal way to prepare the horse physically to carry weight, and is also good mental discipline. It teaches the horse correct responses to the bridle, improves his coordination, and strengthens his trot.

Sometime after the horse turns two or two-and-a-half he begins to carry a rider. Prior to this time carrying weight could be harmful to the young horse's legs and back. Though the horse may appear to be large and strong, a horse younger than 24 months is unable physiologically or psychologically to handle weight under saddle.

By the time the horse is three years old it is being ridden regularly. It is well trained under saddle, physically well muscled, but supple. It responds willingly to all the rider's aids—hands, voice, legs, seat, spur and crop—and takes up the walk and trot on cue. Saddlebreds possessing the correct conformation and inherited inclination will have also been taught to rack. Usually such a horse is not cantered under saddle until it is racking well.

There are nearly as many different ways to develop a Saddlebred's rack as there are trainers who do it. Most of these methods share one thing in common: they all are means of interrupting the horse's natural rhythm at the trot. The job of gaiting a horse is accomplished with the animal under saddle. One method commonly employed is to take the horse outdoors and work him in the trot on a downhill incline. As the horse trots downhill, the rider swings the horse's head from side to side, to break up the rhythm of the square trotting gait. Some horses break into a singlefoot (or pacing) gait almost immediately. If the horse's strong inclination is for a true lateral pace, then the rider needs to employ methods to prevent this. A horse that learns to pace may habitually take up this gait whenever tired, since it requires far less muscular activity from the back and hindquarters.

Some horses need to be worked for weeks before there is any tendency to do anything other than trot, some never learn to rack. Of those who do, not all respond to the above training method—nor any other. What works for one horse is anathema to another. Also, preparation for this work, usually in the form of suppling the horse's neck and body, is performed by the trainer before the gaiting work begins.

The point to be stressed is that while most any dedicated rider may work to improve the action of a naturally gaited horse, anyone attempting to train a horse to gait must be tactful and experienced. Most trainers of five-gaited Saddlebreds spend years as apprentices and journeymen to more experienced horsemen. Real long-term physical and psychological harm may result from the use of inappropriate riding and training methods (and devices).

Once the horse has been taught to singlefoot, the trainer works in an enclosed area to teach it to perform both the rack and the stepping pace, in good form, with high leg action. Once this has been accomplished, he begins to ask the horse for more and more speed at the rack, and more and more slow collection at the stepping pace. All the while, it is important that the horse be worked regularly in a good, strong trot; otherwise there is the possibility of the horse losing his trot altogether. This would make the horse valueless as a five-gaited show horse.

The last show gait that the horse is taught is the canter. Since this is a natural gait, the trainer's job is to teach the horse to perform it in correct form.

Generally this means asking the cantering horse for greater and greater collection, at less and less speed.

5-GAITED SHOW GAITS

While it requires a talented and experienced horse trainer to train a five-gaited Saddlebred, most of us can easily learn to ride a five-gaited horse. The most reliable and fun way to learn about this kind of riding is to attend shows and demonstrations yourself. Then, if your interest is sufficiently piqued, you may want to arrange for saddle seat riding lessons from a qualified instructor at a Saddlebred barn.

THE WALK

When the judge of a five-gaited Saddlebred class calls out "walk," the gait performed by this spirited, graceful horse bears little resemblance to the flat-footed walk of, say, a stock-type horse. Rather, the Saddlebred show ring walk demonstrates impulsion, high leg action, and lightness. His neck is arched proudly, and his tail carried high. This is the typical five-gaited Saddlebred's animated prancing walk. This gait is slightly lateral, performed with correct walking cadence and footfalls.

THE SADDLEBRED TROT

The Saddlebred's trot is animated and evenly cadenced, with diagonal sets of feet landing precisely together. There is a considerable amount of suspension to this trot; this is, however, not as difficult to ride as might be expected, due to the shock absorbing action of the Saddlebred's long, sloping shoulder and pastern, and the rounded, athletic action of his back and hindquarters.

THE SADDLEBRED RACK

A good racking Saddlebred is truly a sight to behold. The animal moves at an such an incredible rate of speed—while still maintaining good overall form, or a proud silhouette—that his legs, all flashing forward independently of one another, actually appear as a blur to the spectator.

Most professional photos of Saddlebreds depict the horse at the trot. Here is a shot of a perfect 4-beat rack, performed by the Saddlebred Beloved Belinda, Joan Robinson Hill up.

While the racking Saddlebred's body appears to be in a frenzy of all-over motion, in truth the concussion of the legs is absorbed so efficiently through the rest of the animal's body that the rider's seat remains unaffected and motionless. The rack is the smoothest, fastest and most exhilarating gait for the rider—but by far the most difficult and exhausting for the horse. Only horses in peak physical condition should be called upon to sustain this gait for more than a very short distance. As with most things, the ecstacy of the rack is fleeting!

SLOW GAIT (STEPPING PACE)

Though it used to be acceptable for horses to show at either the fox trot or the stepping pace when slow gaiting, in today's show ring only the latter is allowed.

The stepping pace as performed in the show ring should be a slow, high-action gait with the emphasis on precision and form. This gait contrasts dramatically with the fast and flashy show rack, thereby offering the horse a perfect opportunity to demonstrate versatility. It is usually a comfortable gait for the rider, as there is little or no suspension between footfalls.

THE CANTER

The Saddlebred's show ring canter is a high, rolling, slow gait that demonstrates both beauty and power. A good Saddlebred show ring canter is a marvel. The feel of a powerful, collected canter from the saddle may be likened to that of a ship rolling up and down on the crest of strong waves. An accomplished rider, like a good sailor, will have developed excellent "sea legs." To such a horseman this gait is as much of a delight to ride as it is to watch.

SHOW RING STYLE

As mentioned earlier, Saddlebreds are shown in the five-gaited division under saddle seat saddles, and with double bridles. Their tails are set, and often they wear protective quarter boots. They never enter the show ring with martingales or any other types of head setting devices.

Five-gaited horses are shown with a full mane and tail, with a long braided ribbon attached to the horse's forelock and mane at the foretop.

Five-gaited riders wear formal saddle seat attire, meaning a long, well-tailored greatcoat with matching pants, a light colored shirt, vest, and tie. A derby hat for ladies and a snap brim hat for gentlemen finishes the look. While basic show ring attire should always be well-fitting and in good taste, some brilliant color—red, yellow, green, royal or bright blue—is often displayed in vests, ties or in ladies' coats. For effect, the same color may be mirrored on the horse's patent-leather show bridle. These folks are, after all, in "show business!"

WORLD'S CHAMPIONSHIP HORSE SHOW

Early in this century many prominent horse shows claimed World's Championships for Saddlebreds. In 1916 a movement was begun by Jumps

HEAVENLY GAITS

Cauthorn, a Missouri magazine editor, to settle on one five-gaited World's Champion by means of a $10,000 stakes class. He requested that such a class be held at the Missouri State Fair.

When the governor of Missouri turned this request down, Mat Cohen, Kentucky's Commissioner of Agriculture, took up the cause from his friend Cauthorn. Cauthorn and other horsemen had already raised half the needed money, Mat Cohen helped to raise the rest. In 1917 the first official World's Championship was held at the Kentucky State Fair. Only five-gaited horses competed for the World's Championship title at this first competition; three-gaited and harness classes weren't added until twenty years later.

CONTEMPORARY HORSE SHOWS

Most county fairs, as well as many riding clubs and regional Saddlebred associations throughout the U.S., sponsor horse shows with a five-gaited Saddlebred division. Some of the people who compete in these shows eventually move up to exhibiting in the larger and more prestigious shows. Competing the Saddlebred at any level or division is an exciting pastime. But to some owners, riders, and trainers nothing compares to exhibiting a horse with the beauty, talent and training to stand up to some of the best competitive five-gaited Saddlebreds in the world.

This level of competition is demonstrated at many major shows throughout the United States. The most prestigious is still the Kentucky State Fair World's Championship Horse Show held each year in Louisville, Kentucky. The American Royal is another prestigious show still being held each year in Kansas City, Missouri. A few other such shows are the National Horse Show, now at The Meadowlands in New Jersey; the Devon Horse Show, at Devon, Pennsylvania; and The Pin Oak Charity Show in Houston, Texas. All of the great state fairs—Iowa, Missouri, Illinois, Indiana, Ohio, Michigan, Texas, etc.—boast prominent five-gaited Saddlebred divisions. The Lexington Junior League Horse Show in Lexington, Kentucky claims to be the nation's biggest outdoor show featuring American Saddlebreds. Following is a list of shows around the U.S. that have five-gaited Grand National Saddlebred classes.

Del Mar Charity Horse Show, Del Mar, CA
Denver Queen City Horse Show, Denver, CO
Southeastern Charity Horse Show, Alpharetta, GA
River City Classic, Evansville, IL
Midwest Charity show, Springfield, IL
Indy 500, Indianapolis, IN
Kentucky Fall Classic; Lexington, KY
Rock Creek Horse Show, Louisville, KY
Dixie Jubilee Horse Show; Baton Rouge, LA
Eastern States Horse Show, W. Springfield, MA
St. Louis National Horse Show, St. Louis, MO
All American Classic Horse Show, Indianapolis, MN
Tanbark Cavalcade of Roses, St. Paul, MN
Blowing Rock Charity Show, Blowing Rock, NC
Nebraska State Charity Show, Lincoln, NE
National Horse Show; New York, NY
Syracuse International, Syracuse, NY
Dayton Horse Show, Dayton, OH
Northwest Saddlebred Association Fall Classic; Eugene, OR
Lawrence County Charity Show, New Castle, PA
Germantown Charity Horse Show, Germantown, TN
Music City Horse Show, Nashville, TN
Roanoke Valley Horse Show, Roanoke, VA

CH—CHAMPIONS

Horses who accumulate enough points at these and other shows recognized by the ASHA are given the official designation CH (for Champion). This is why we now read about CH My-My, CH Wing Commander, CH Imperator, etc. While it isn't necessary to win the five-gaited World's Championship to earn this title, only the best show horses in the nation are honored with this official name change.

The American Saddle Horse Museum at Kentucky Horse Park in

HEAVENLY GAITS

Lexington, Kentucky keeps excellent written, video, statuary and pictorial records of all the well-known and acclaimed Saddlebreds. Anyone interested in this breed of horse will learn a great deal by visiting this historical museum.

SADDLEBRED HORSE SALES

In the early 1800's through the early part of this century, people used to go to the county seat on circuit court day, or else to the county fair, to make horse swapping deals. During the past half century, however, another Saddlebred tradition has evolved: the Saddlebred horse auction.

Many large Saddlebred farms hold annual production sales. Other sales are sponsored by commercial auction companies. One of the oldest and best-known of the latter is Tattersalls, in Lexington, Kentucky. Tattersalls, the oldest light horse market in the U.S., celebrated its centennial in 1992.

Though much has changed in the horse sale business, some things remain the same. As in the early days of the "Kentucky Saddler," people still travel great distances to see—and to purchase—a good quality American Saddlebred. This graceful horse still makes a grand appearance in the sale ring, and people still shake with anticipation as he is introduced to the crowd:

"LADIES AND GENTLEMEN, we have here before us a magnificent horse, with some of the oldest and best bloodlines in the country coursing through his veins. . ."

Thus, from generation to generation, people from all walks of life are sold on the versatility, intelligence and beauty of the American Saddlebred.

—Chapter Three—
The Tennessee Walking Horse

It's little wonder that people involved with the Tennessee Walking Horse often wax romantic when talking about their horses. A well bred Tennessee Walking Horse possesses style, strength, stamina, speed, smooth saddle gaits, versatility and an easy-going temperament. This is because the Tennessee Walking Horse is the result of crossing several breeds and types of horses, each known for possessing a particular quality that was especially valued by Americans who depended upon their horses—often more than they depended upon one another.

Every kind of horse that was valued by the early Americans went into the makeup of the horse that originated in Middle Tennessee. Horses of that era and region provided their owners with everyday transportation, both under saddle and as carriage horses. Horses helped pioneers to clear heavily forested lands, and then provided the necessary horsepower to plow, cultivate, plant, inspect and harvest crops from it. Then it was their job to pull heavily laden wagons to distant markets. When colonists became work-weary, their horses provided them with all kinds of entertainment—in the show and sales arenas of the day, in pulling contests that pitted one horse's strength against another, and on the numerous roads and racetracks that were hewn out of the land—also by horses. Horses carried men into war, and helped to rebuild the nation when the war was over. They transported the mail, carried country doctors and midwives into homestead areas, pulled the fire wagons, and brought the circuit judges and preachers to town. Their financial value contributed to the economic prosperity of America even while their spirits and personalities substantially enriched the personal lives of its people.

Out of this virile culture of horsemanship rose the Tennessee Walking Horse.

MIDDLE TENNESSEE AND ITS HORSES

The natural resources of middle Tennessee were so rich that several Indian tribes east of the Mississippi honored an ancient agreement reserving the area as an unpossessed hunting ground. Its abundant wild game could be shared by all, its land was to be settled by none. White men changed all that in 1780, when they moved south from Virginia and founded Nashville. This was no easy task, as early settlers faced the ire of those Indians who resisted their encroachment upon the productive forests of the region. Native Americans fought desperately to keep their hunting grounds uncleared and unsettled—but to no avail. One of the advantages the white settlers had were good horses. The horses these first settlers brought with them had to be swift, sure-footed, strong and possessed of great courage and endurance. The animals used were built upon a foundation of Narragansett, Thoroughbred and Morgan breeding, as were most of the horses of the early colonists.

Many strains of American horses during our early history boasted great speed, since it was a popular practice to breed horses for racing. In the 1700's men raced their horses under saddle. Most of these were trotting horses (of Thoroughbred and Morgan blood) since riding a pacer at wide-open speeds was nearly impossible.

EARLY PACING STOCK

As roadways improved, men began hitching their fastest horses to wagons, sleds, and carts. This led to the advent of race courses and, eventually, the racing cart. Once race horses no longer had to be ridden, pacing horses, and pacing horse races, began to receive wider acceptance. Pacers usually set faster times, or standards, than did the trotters. In the mid 1800's the standard of time for running a mile was about 2 minutes, 30 seconds. Standards were gradually lowered as horses, and courses, improved. Horses who met or exceeded the standard were eligible for registration in the U.S. Trotting Association. By 1879 horses who met or exceeded the standard one mile race time and were registered with the U.S. Trotting Association came to be known as Standardbreds. Many great Standardbreds stand behind the foundation lines of the Tennessee Walking Horse

By 1810 Middle Tennessee boasted several racing tracks over which both trotting and pacing races were run. By this time trotting and pacing stock was commonly imported into the region for racing, and the Tennessee Walking Horse owes much of its foundation blood to these early race horses —Thoroughbred (at the time merely called "blood" horses), Trotting horses, and Canadian Pacers. The latter are considered by many to be nothing other than the Narragansett Pacer, as a great many of them were exported from the United States to Canada. A number of Canadian Pacers that were imported into Middle Tennessee during the early 1800's exerted an especially strong influence on early Tennessee horse breeding. When these Canadian horses were crossed with native Tennessee mares, they produced a type of horse that became widely known as the Tennessee Pacer.

It is only to be expected that some of the sires that were influential in the development of the American Saddle Horse would also contribute to the type of horse being developed in Middle Tennessee, and Canadian Pacers were no exception. Canadian Pacers who made significant contributions to both the American Saddle Horse and the Tennessee Pacer were Copperbottom, Old Pilot, Davy Crockett and Tom Hal.

Copperbottom was a coppery-colored sorrel, known for producing fast pacing stock, "extremely stout and well made." It has been surmised that his blood was used to overcome too much "trottiness" in the saddle horses of the era, a result of early breeders relying too heavily upon Thoroughbred racing blood. Americans from the south wanted speed—but unlike their eastern counterparts, they also had high regard for the smooth saddle gaited horses. Copperbottom was therefore ideal for use on their mares, as he was reputed to produce smooth riding horses who could also run. An advertisement for Copperbottom's breeding services that was run in the June 10, 1816 issue of the Lexington, Kentucky newspaper claimed he could run in harness, while pulling two men, over a 16-1/2 mile distance in just one hour. It was further claimed that he could outrun any horse in Kentucky over a race course one to four miles long.

Another family of horses that were extremely significant to the Tennessee Walking Horse were the Tom Hal's. These horses, thought to originate with a pacing horse named Tom Hal that was foaled in Canada in 1802, were brought to Middle Tennessee in large numbers after the civil war. There they gained a reputation for being incredibly strong, versatile and docile animals with smooth riding gaits. Tom Hal horses played no small role in the post-civil war reconstruction of the south.

That's not where the Tom Hal contribution ends. In 1836 a Copperbottom mare was bred with the original Tom Hal (who by now was in his mid-thirties), and in 1837 that union produced Bald Stockings, the first horse on record to perform the running walk. Bald Stockings was a roan horse with four white feet and a bald face. This stallion became known for being one of the fastest, smoothest riding horses of his day, as well as a prepotent sire. One of his most influential offspring was Queen, a mare who became the dam of Latham's Denmark, Diamond Denmark, and King William (who was great grandsire to Roan Allen F-38, one of the great foundation sires of the Tennessee Walking Horse). In addition to this, Bald Stockings was the direct grandsire of a horse that was named Gibson's Tom Hal, later to be designated Tom Hal F-20. This horse was considered so important to the foundation breeding of the Tennessee Walking Horse that he was a serious contender for the designation of Tom Hal F-1—the breed's most important early sire.

The Copperbottom family of horses were the progenitors of a family of horses known as the Mountain Slashers. This family of grey horses, whose blood would enter the mainstream of the modern day Tennessee Walking Horse through several foundation horses, also possessed smooth saddle gaits and speed.

The Grey Johns—particularly a horse named Boone's Grey John—was another family of horses significant to the development of the walking horse. It is believed by most breed historians that Boone's Grey John came from Copperbottom breeding, though establishing this has been difficult due to his early history. During the civil war a Yankee left a pregnant, exhausted Saddle

Horse mare at the farm of Capt. Nathan Boone's farm, in Boonesville, Tennessee. The foal she bore was called Boone's Grey John. This stallion was the fountainhead for a family of horses who became highly valued for their fast, smooth running walk and their remarkable good sense. Grey John was reputed to be able to perform a perfect running walk at the rate of eight miles per hour. He also sired horses with remarkable speed and gaits. One of Boones Grey John's sons, Buford L, became a foundation sire for the Tennessee Walking Horse—as did a stallion named Bramlett, by Buford L. For two years Bramlett stood in Texas, and undoubtedly played a significant role in the early origins of the Tennessee Walking Horse in that state.

Davy Crockett was a Canadian Pacer brought to the U.S. around 1840. He sired Brinker's Drennon, who appears in the pedigree of Gertrude, one of the Tennessee Walking Horse's most significant foundation mares.

The most important contribution of the Canadian Pacer known as Pacing Pilot (or Old Pilot) to the Tennessee Walker was through Earnhart's Brooks, who was foaled around 1875 near Shelbyville, Tennessee. Jimmy Joe Murray, an avid and knowledgeable promoter of the Tennessee Walking Horse during the early 1900's wrote:

> *"Of all the Foundation Stock upon which the noble ancestry of the Tennessee Walking Horse is based, perhaps none is more basically sound or highly prized than the renowned blood which has been contributed to the breed by Earnhart's Brooks. . .we venture to assert that 75% of Registered Tennessee Walking Horses have more Earnhart's Brooks blood than any other Foundation Stallion—with the exception of Allan F-1."*

TROTTING HORSE CONTRIBUTIONS

Besides pacing stock, a number of trotting horses made important contributions to the foundation lines of the Tennessee Walking Horse. Among these was the Bullet family, which traces its roots to Morgan stock. Thoroughbred blood was contributed through horses like the imported Whip, and McMeen's Traveler. The latter was especially influential in the development of horses in Middle Tennessee. McMeen's Traveler breeding was so popular during the civil war that members of the Confederate army deliberately set out to find these horses to use as calvary mounts. It is reported that forty-seven of them were included among Nathan Bedford Forrest's regiment of soldiers, and that due to their swiftness and good sense none were ever lost in action. McMeen's Traveler sired many great sons and daughters, many who went on to become celebrities in their own right. Joe Bowers and Prince Pulaski, two sons of McMeen's Traveler, are very important to the foundation breeding of the Tennessee Walking Horse.

The Mountain Slashers are believed to have carried a mixture of Copperbottom and Thoroughbred blood, this mixture creating a unique formula for smoothness and speed. The original Mountain Slasher had such a smooth and fast racing pace that in an autobiography account by "Pop" Geers (known as the "Grand Old Man of Racing"), we can read of a race on "First Monday," or county circuit day, in which Mountain Slasher was ridden by William Goldson. Part of this account reads as follows:

> *"When they were ready, Goldston placed the riding whip in his mouth, dropped the bridle rein on Slasher's neck, placed his hands on his hip and, with arms akimbo, started with the others; and on they came, Goldston sitting as erect as a piece of statuary, and every little while sticking the spurs into the sides of Slasher, who with the reins lying loose on his neck, and without anything to steady him except his inherent pacing instinct, regardless of stones and the rough uneven surface, never broke his true even pace, and clearly outpaced all his competitors and carried off the laurels of the day."*

FOUNDATION SIRE

Out of this pool of excellent pacing and trotting blood emerged a horse that would become the progenitor of The Tennessee Walking Horse we know today. This horse was a black stallion who was originally known simply as Allan. Later he would be called Black Allan. Later still he was designated Allan F-1.

In the early 1880's George Ely, a man from Ohio, purchased a trotting race stallion from Lexington, Kentucky. This horse, who became known as Elyria, was an 1882 foal by the great Mambrino King, and out of the dam Maggie Marshall. Ely was so impressed by Elyria's speed that he returned to Lexington in 1886 to purchase his dam, Maggie Marshall, who by that time had a black pacing colt at her side. The colt was Allan, who was bred by an E.H. Kerr, and was sired by the popular stallion Allandorf.

Because Elyria was a very fast trotting race horse, Ely fully expected Maggie's colt to develop into a talented trotter. Despite Ely's best training efforts, Maggie's colt insisted on pacing at speed. Historical perspective offers us the reason for this: Onward, Allan's grandsire, was the sire of more than two hundred horses who could race the standard time of 2:30; one hundred thirty-five of these Onward horses were pacers.

Since pacing horses were in low demand, particularly in the east, Ely sent the black horse, who was by then six years old, to Tattersalls sale in Lexington, Kentucky. There Allan was sold to John B. Mankin, of Murfreesboro, Tennessee for $335—twenty dollars less than the recorded average price of horses at that day's sale.

Allan stood barely over fifteen hands, and though he possessed speed, his gaits were so loose that he failed to finish well in races. J.E. McDonald, Mankin's trainer's, said that Allan was one of the easiest horses he ever worked with. But "easy" wasn't one of the most important qualities people looked for in a horse—speed was. McDonald's training failed to result in any improvement in squaring up his gaits, or in increasing his speed. When Allan proved unsuccessful as a race horse, he was relegated to the barn to serve at stud.

There being many popular sires standing in Middle Tennessee during that time, Allan faced a great deal of competition. Since few people from Tennessee were looking for a small pacing horse who never measured up to the competition for speed, Allan had few takers as a sire. This resulted in his being sold several more times, at ever decreasing prices.

Though Allan failed to catch the world's—or even the region's— attention as a sire during his prime, he must have been recognized as a quality horse by the people who owned and managed him, as he was never gelded. W.J. McGill, a man from Shelbyville, Tennessee, was Allan's official biographer, and his research verifies that Allan F-1 was a horse with obvious quality. After many years of painstaking research, McGill pieced together the history of, and facts concerning, Allan F-1. According to an article by him in a 1945 issue of *The Blue Ribbon* magazine, Allan:

> *". . .had smart ears, a perfect head, wonderful eyes, full and well-set body, a long rangy neck, beautiful mane and foretop, a divided sloping shoulder, and a breast that belongs to an outstanding Tennessee Walking Horse.*
>
> *"He had fine body lines, a short back, a long belly, was well coupled, smooth hips and rump, a natural set long wavy tail. The abundant style he shows in head and neck, smooth limbs, cordy muscles, good foot and bone, his superb gaits, his easy, graceful way of going into the fast running walk, justify our statement that he was as fine as they make him."*

In 1903 Allan ended up in the hands of Mr. James R. Brantley of Coffee County, Tennessee. The aged stallion had been sold or traded no less than eight times since leaving Mankin's hands. Brantley himself received Allan only as a by-product of a donkey-buying deal. He was asked to pay $400 for a fine black jack owned by J.A. McCulloch, and the latter offered Allan for an additional $110 (which modest sum was more than Allan had brought in other horse buying/trading deals). Known as "The Old Teaser," Allan was being used by McCulloch to tease mares in preparation for being bred to his jack. A more inglorious job for a stallion could hardly be imagined.

On the face of it there was certainly little reason for James Brantley to want to own such a horse. But Brantley was a student of horse genealogies and, probably prompted by Allan's fine appearance, decided to check out the horse's pedigree before making his decision. Brantley traveled over 100 miles while tracing Allan's history. He discovered Allan's registration in the American Trotting Horse Register, where he learned that Allandorf was Allan's sire. Allandorf was a top breeding stallion by Onward and out of a mare named Dolly. The register stated that Onward was the grandest stallion, living or dead. Both Onward and Dolly had pedigrees that read like a "Who's Who" of top colonial breeding. His sire boasted the blood of the famous horses Alma

Allan F-1, primary foundation sire of the Tennessee Walking Horse.

Photo Courtesy of Harry Bosley

Mater, Onward, Mambrino Patchen, George Wilkes, and Hambletonian 10 (through whom he traced to the great Thoroughbred Messenger, foundation sire for the Standardbred horse). Allan traced twice to the great Mambrino Chief, a trotting horse (also of Messenger breeding) whose blood helped to establish the Saddle Horse family. Allan's dam, Maggie Marshall, was also well bred with lines tracing to the great Morgan horses Bradford's Telegraph, Black Hawk, Sherman Morgan and Justin Morgan.Besides this, Maggie's other offspring had gained reputations as great race horses.

It would have been obvious to any student of horse breeding that Allan traced to a majority of the best breeding lines in America. Some of his ancestors were known for speed, some for beauty and still others for outstanding saddle gaits—in short, these horses were the epitome of the finest qualities of every type of horse in the nation. A firm believer in the value of fine blood, James Brantley hitched up his favorite mare, Gertrude, to a buggy and set out for McCulloch's house to close the deal. Then he hooked Allan to the buggy, tied the jack to the back of the conveyance, and, with a neighbor riding Gertrude alongside the buggy, made the two day trip to his home in Beech Grove, Tennessee.

Under Brantley's management the fine black stallion finally got the recognition he had so long deserved. He was used to breed the owner's walking horse mares, including Gertrude, who boasted the blood of Queen, by Bald Stockings, by Tom Hal. Bald Stockings was the first horse ever to demonstrate the running walk; his dam Queen also produced several very important early Saddle Horse sires. Besides Queen and Bald Stockings, Gertrude carried the blood of Artist, King William, Washington Denmark, Davy Crockett, Brinker's Drennon, Bullett and Earnhart's Brooks. It would be hard to imagine any two horses with finer pedigrees than Allan and Gertrude. Not surprisingly the product of their union, Roan Allen, would indelibly stamp Allan's mark on future generations of walking horses.

At James Brantley's, Allan's services were also used on some of Middle Tennessee's other finely bred mares, many boasting blood from the Morgans, Denmarks, Copperbottoms, Stonewalls, Mountain Slashers, Tom Hals, Brooks, Bullets, Boone's Grey John's, Whips, and most of the other quality bred horses for that period. Much of the breeding was the same being used in the makeup of the American Saddle Horse.Unlike the Saddle Horse breeders of that period, whose horses often had only an inclination for saddle gaits that was developed through training, people from Middle Tennessee were beginning to breed individual horses with an eye to reproducing naturally occurring saddle gaits, especially the running walk.

In fact, it was during this time that the two types of horses began to become distinct from one another. This is because the Saddle Horse people were line breeding to Denmark horses; shortly thereafter Tennessee Walking Horse people began line breeding to the Allan family. But breeders of walking horses---the name given this new type of horse—never limited themselves to Allan blood. They continued to include outside influences in their efforts to improve and refine their breed. Because so many strains of types of animals were used in the creation of the Tennessee Walking Horse, the registry lists 115 foundation horses.

Besides holding court for a number of blue-blooded "ladies," Allan was valued as a good all-around family horse. French Brantley, the owner's son, rode the gentle stud to school every morning, and left him tied to a tree all day. French's friends often ran Allan in impromptu races, where he gained a reputation for being able to pace as fast as most horses could gallop.

From James Brantley himself comes the following description of Allan

F-1, as he told it in a 1945 issue of *The Blue Ribbon*, just before his death at age 83:

> *"Allan F-1 was as easy-gaited a horse as anyone ever rode. I rode him myself, and so did my children and many neighbors. No stallion ever lived who had a better disposition. His gaits in the trot, pace, flat or running walk were perfect. He had a particular gliding gait under saddle, truly equal to the family rocking chair. He had perfect style, a very high head, a natural, high tail, quick, very fine hair, good flat bone and ample foot. Indeed, anyone today would have to appraise him as a great horse, which he was."*

At James Brantley's, Black Allan became renowned as an outstanding sire of smooth gaited saddle horses. Allan so consistently passed on his easy gliding gait—and, through his son, Roan Allen, proved that his get could do the same—that he eventually came to the attention of Albert M. Dement of Wartrace, Tennessee. By this time Roan Allen, Allan's son out of Gertrude, was such a popular sire that James Brantley now had little call for the older stallion's services. So he allowed his friend Dement—who would become known as an all time great breeder of walking horses—to purchase Allan in 1909 for $140. Allan was moved to the Dement farm, about ten miles away from Brantley's. This was a decision that James Brantley later deeply regretted. The agreement between the two breeders was that the stallion would live through the next breeding season—which is precisely what the honest old stallion did. After servicing no fewer than 111 mares during a seven month period, Allan died in September, 1910. Dement's trainer Jack Grider wrote in the Dement stud book:

> *"September 16, 1910. Allan died. Served 111 mares and is said to be 29 years old and he never did have a missing tooth. He was the gamest horse I ever saw."*

Though by the time he died—he was actually 24 years old—Allan had gained a reputation as a sire of good horses, it would be many more years before Allan F-1 was recognized as one of the nation's most prepotent, influential American horse sires. It would be hard to imagine what the outcome might have been for American horses had Allan not been lost as a sire during his first seventeen years. Through the offspring of his later years, Allan's place in history became assured. When the Tennessee Walking Horse Breeder's Association was formed in 1935, Allan's contribution to the breed was honored when he was given the title Allan F-1—the first designated foundation sire for the Tennessee Walking Horse. Out of a large number of truly great horses, Allan F-1 was the greatest of them all.

While Allan sired many great horses during his years as a popular stud, over the years two have stood out above the others. These were Roan Allen F-38 and Hunter's Allen F-10. (No one is quite sure why the spelling of Allan was changed to Allen with succeeding generations.)

ROAN ALLEN F-38

Of all of Allan F-1's get, the son whose name was destined to become synonymous with the term *walking horse* was Roan Allen, the 1904 foal out of James Brantley's great mare Gertrude. This 15.3 hand, extremely masculine red roan stallion proved to be so prepotent, and was a remarkably popular show horse and sire during his lifetime. Roan Allen had the ability to sire not only outstanding stallions, but excellent and prepotent daughters, as well.

Roan Allen himself was an unusually versatile horse. Besides being able to perform a superb natural running walk, he was put into training with Charlie Ashley of Manchester, Tennessee, where he was trained to perform every popular gait of the period. This included the flat walk, running walk, rack, fox walk, fox trot and square trot. He also proved to be a good horse under harness. Roan Allen's versatility was proved again and again in the show rings, when he would compete and win against the top horses of Middle Tennessee in gaited horse classes, walking horse classes and combination classes—the latter being a class where a horse was first driven to harness and then ridden under saddle. This popular stud horse was also competed in children's classes, where he demonstrated that he inherited his sire's kind

Photo courtesy of Harry Bosley

Roan Allen F-38 was a flashy red roan who was so strongly gaited that he performed every saddle gait to perfection.

---

disposition, as well as his talents. James Brantley said about Roan Allen:

"Frankly, I always gave him credit for having abundant brains, and I still consider him the smartest horse, with the best disposition, of any horse I have ever known."

In 1945 Henry Davis wrote that Roan Allen was competing on the 1911 and 1912 county fair circuit at Murfreesboro, Tullahoma, Fayetteville, Winchester and the Tennessee State Fair in Nashville. About these competitions he wrote:

"This circuit. . .brought out all of the best horses in Tennessee. There were as many great gaited, harness and walking horses at this time as were ever shown before or since. . .no horse I have ever known could do a more perfect rack than Roan Allen. His pomp and style, erect head, the longest and most perfect neck on any horse, perfectly arched, erect ears, and a heavy water sprout flaxen tail that would touch the ground when he was standing still, made him what I still consider to be a perfect picture of horse flesh."

HEAVENLY GAITS

ROAN ALLEN OFFSPRING: GENERAL

It was only natural that, once Roan Allen's own first foals hit the ground and proved his ability to sire horses with his own outstanding qualities, people flocked to the James Brantley farm from all over the south to breed their best brood mares to the son of Black Allan. While some of his sons and daughters followed Roan Allen into the show ring, many others were valued for their distinctive running walk, and were sold as walking horses to large plantation owners in Mississippi, Arkansas and Louisiana. Thirty Roan Allen stallion sons are registered in the Tennessee Walking Horse Breeder's and Exhibitor's Association, and the majority of these outstanding horses sired other outstanding horses, as judged by their show ring records. The two Roan Allen's sons who would become the most influential sires of the breed, Wilson's Allen and Merry Boy, were nearly both lost to obscurity during their lifetimes. Their stories each illustrate the role that destiny seems to play in the lives of great horses.

WILSON'S ALLEN

One of Roan Allen's top show horse producing sons was Wilson's Allen. This horse was foaled on the Bud Messick farm in Coffee County, Tennessee in 1915, out of the mare Birdie Messick, by Allan F-1. Wilson's Allen the first line bred Allen horse, since his grandsire on both sides was Allan F-1. Bud Messick was unimpressed by the foal, and sold him to a man named Johnson Hill when the colt was just one day old. Hill took possession of the weanling in the fall, and he became known as the Johnson Hill Horse.

At three years of age the horse was placed in training with John Parker in Shelbyville, Tennessee. Parker liked the stallion's gentle nature and excellent walking horse gait, and in 1918 placed him in the only show of his lifetime, where the young stallion took second place honors behind Merry King, a son of Albert Dement's famed mare, Merry Legs.

Unwilling to keep paying the trainer's fee of $15 per month, Johnson Hill took the horse back home to his farm in Beech Grove, Tennessee, where he was put to farm work until 1923, a year after Hill's death.

At some point during that time the great stallion lost an eye in a farm accident. This did not prevent Bibb Kirby from Tennessee's Bedford County from seeing the potential of the eight-year-old stallion when he was offered for sale in 1923. Kirby bought the one-eyed stallion, and did his best to promote him as a sire, but mostly to no avail. During the next five years Kirby's efforts only resulted in the birth of two really great plantation walking horses. One of these was Haynes Peacock, a gelding who became the first two-time winner of the World Grand Championship; the other was a stallion named Slippery Allen, who was to become a top show horse and sire.

In 1928 Bibb Kirby, who had little time to care for the stallion, reluctantly sold him to Frank Wilson of Pelham, Tennessee for $150. Under Wilson's apt promotion and management the thirteen year old stallion—now known as Wilson's Allen—finally became a popular sire and was used on a number of good quality brood mares, not only those from Middle Tennessee, but from all over the south. One of his most famous sons, Pride of Memphis, was foaled in 1932, and it was largely through him that Wilson Allen gained his reputation as a sire of great walking horses. Had it not been for Frank Wilson, Wilson's Allen's name would almost surely have been lost to the walking horse world.

As it is, his name appears in the pedigrees of many World Grand Champions, including Midnight Sun, the 1945 and 1946 World Grand Champion whose record as a top sire of Tennessee Walking Horse show champions may never be surpassed.

Wilson Allen's son Midnight Sun sired Midnight Merry, World Grand Champion of 1949; Talk of the Town, World Grand Champion of 1951, 1952 and 1953; Sun's Jet Parade, World Grand Champion of 1957; Setting Sun, World Grand Champion of 1958; and Sun's Delight D., 1963 World Grand Champion. Midnight Sun also sired two of the modern day's most significant show horse sires: Ebony Masterpiece and Pride of Midnight. Both of these stallions sired four World Grand Champions. Ebony's Masterpiece was sire of World Grand Champions Another Masterpiece, 1974; Ebony's True Grit, 1975; Ebony's Mountain Man, 1980; and Ebony's Bold Courier, 1983). Pride of Midnight sired World Grand Champions Pride's Secret Threat, 1982; Delight of Pride, 1984; Pride's Final Edition, 1985; and Pride's Jubilee Star, 1986.

HEAVENLY GAITS

As mentioned earlier, Wilson's Allen also sired good daughters, including the famous Maude Gray, one of the all-time great show horse producing plantation walking horse brood mares. Unfortunately, the names of the dams of great horses are often buried in a pedigree, so that a sire becomes famous by virtue of the sons he produces.

One of the tragedies in the history of the Tennessee Walking Horse is that so many of Wilson's Allen's outstanding sons were gelded before they attained recognition. Four such great show geldings by Wilson's Allen were Pride of Memphis, The G-Man, Strolling Jim (1939 World Grand Champion) and Haynes Peacock, who held the title of World Grand Champion in 1940 and 1941.

Horses with Wilson's Allen breeding, valued for their outstanding boldness and graceful, loose gaits, have consistently placed in the top show rings of the nation from the time the great horse's name first became known until the present day.

MERRY BOY

Another great son of Roan Allen was Merry Boy, a 1945 foal out of the Albert Dement mare Merry Legs. Starting in the early 1900's Albert Dement instituted a daring program of line breeding that resulted in his horses becoming the plantation walking horse's most prepotent stock, which eventually led to breeders being able to consistently reproduce the running walk through successive generations. Merry Legs, who was Merry Boy's dam, was an extraordinarily successful product of this breeding program; she not only was a very successful show horse herself, but is listed on the pedigrees of more National Celebration show winning stock than any other broodmare, being named on the dam's side of more than a dozen World Grand Champions.

Though her son Merry Boy was only known to win one blue ribbon in his life—and that at a small regional show as a two year old—many of Merry Legs greatest progeny come through her son Merry Boy, by Roan Allen F-38. This is hardly less than a minor miracle since Merry Boy's uneven black roan coloring combined with an extreme and clearly demonstrated dislike for being ridden caused him to be underrated as a sire throughout his life. It has

History has shown that Merry Boy, a cantankerous, unevenly colored black roan who was under-rated as a sire in his day, was one of the top-producing sires of the Tennessee Walking Horse.

only been through a study of show records accumulated through the years that Merry Boy has come to be recognized as one of the top producing sires of the Tennessee Walking Horse.

Part of the reason Merry Boy's offspring failed to make a big impression during his lifetime is because they usually were forced to compete in the show ring against the sons and daughters of Wilson's Allen, who were nearly unbeatable in such competition. Also, his get tended to inherit his difficult temperament—and were often white, which was an unpopular color for walking horses.

In spite of these obstacles, Merry Boy did manage to breed some good mares. The result of these is that his name appears among the great show horse sires of The Tennessee Walking Horse. Among his celebrated offspring is Dement's Merry Legs II, out of Skip, a mare who was out of Merry Legs and by the popular stallion Slippery Jim. Dement's Merry Legs II (commonly called Little Merry Legs) became the second three year old to ever win the World Championship class at the Tennessee State Fair, in 1936. The first three-year-old to win it had been Merry Legs, her grand-dam through both Merry Boy and Skip, in 1914. Dement's Merry Legs II repeated her performance the next year. In all, this "Little Merry Legs" competed in forty shows, and took first place ribbons in every one of them.

Most of Merry Boy's offspring were great show horses, but continued to trail behind Wilson's Allen offspring in the show rings of his day. The first notable exception to this rule was Merry Go Boy, a finely built black stallion whose popularity as a sire would far outstrip his sire's. Merry Go Boy won the title of World Grand Champion in 1947 and 1948, and was the sire of three World Champions: Go Boy's Shadow (1955-56); Go Boy's Sundust (1967); and Go Boy's Royal Heir (1968). Through his son, Old Glory, he was grandsire to 1950 World Grand Champion, Old Glory's Big Man.

Besides siring great stallions, Merry Boy is unexcelled as a sire of top brood mares. These included Merry Rose, the dam of three time World Grand Champion Talk of the Town (1951-1953); Merry Walker, dam of World Champions Go Boy's Shadow (1955-56) and Rodger's Perfection (1959); Crain's Merry Lady, dam of World Grand Champion White Star (1954); Merry Sue, dam of World Grand Champion Sun's Jet Parade (1957); and Lady Lee, dam of World Grand Champion Ebony's Masterpiece (1962). Merry Boy's record of producing top brood mares is hardly limited to those who produced World Grand Champions. The complete story of all his daughters' successes would fill a book.

So, while Merry Boy and his get enjoyed limited show ring success during his lifetime, show rings of the future proved him to be the progenitor of many of the world's greatest Tennessee Walking Horses.

HUNTER'S ALLEN F-10

The other influential son by Allan F-1 was Hunter's Allen, a sorrel horse foaled in 1909 out of a mare named Allis. Little certain factual information is available about Allis, but she was a good looking, tall mare who stood sixteen hands high. Her official pedigree traces her to the Copperbottom and Mountain Slasher horse families. It is known for certain that her sire was named Pat, a rather lethargic animal who was once used to pull a whisky peddler's wagon.

In any event, this tall good-looking mare, when bred to Allan F-1, produced a golden sorrel foal with an off hind stocking, a star and snip. This foal nearly didn't make it past day one, when he fell off a bridge onto a flat rock, and lay as though dead. His breeder and owner, J.N. Black, thought so little of the colt that he didn't bother trying to rescue him. Fortunately for Hunter's Allen and the Tennessee Walking Horse world, the gangly colt soon regained his footing and suffered no lasting bad effects from the fall.

Black sold the colt to a J.W. Davis, a small town country storekeeper from Coffee County. While with Davis the young horse was hitched to harness with a pony and used to deliver groceries. At the time he was known as Little Allen.

When Little Allen was not yet three Davis sold him to John Walker, who kept him until he was eight years old. Although old original Tennessee State Fair records were destroyed by fire, historians have been able to reconstruct many of these. Reconstructed records indicate that Walker entered Little Allen in the Tennessee State Fair competitions, where he won the Stallion division of the Tennessee State Fair's Walking Horse classes in 1912, 1913, and 1916.

Walker sold the horse, who had a reputation for being extremely difficult to handle, to Bright Hunter of Farmington, Tennessee. He remained with the Hunter family until his death in 1932, and became known during that time as Hunter's Allen. Though he never shook his reputation for having a nasty temperament, he did become a winning show horse and popular sire during his lifetime. Hunter's Allen's most prominent sons were Brown Allen, Last Chance and Walker's Allen. His blood made its most significant contributions to the modern Tennessee Walking Horse breed through female lines. Ramsey's Rena, dam of Midnight Sun, was his granddaughter, as was the dam Maude Gray, who produced many outstanding and prepotent walking horses.

ALBERT DEMENT: MASTER BREEDER

We've already outlined the role that James Brantley played as the man who recognized the potential of Allan F-1, and was lifetime owner and breeder of the great Roan Allen F-38. Another man at least as important to the breed as James Brantley is Albert Dement, the friend of James Brantley who owned Allan F-1 during the last year of his life. Dement has been designated the Master Breeder of the Tennessee Walking Horse, and not without reason.

At the turn of the century there was no predictability in the breeding of walking horses. Some of the foals from Middle Tennessee stock inherited the natural running walk, others did not. Albert Dement believed it was possible, by means of inbreeding and linebreeding, to develop a line of horses that would consistently demonstrate the desired gait.

Dement was merciless in his judgements about what horses were appropriate for his use: no matter how good a horse was in every other respect, if it failed to produce the desired gait, it was eliminated. Much of his program's eventual success hinged on two mares, Nell Dement and her great walking horse daughter Merry Legs, by Allan F-1.

Nell Dement was a registered Saddle Horse mare that Dement took to

Breed developers James R. Brantley (left) and Albert M. Dement (right). The horse is the famous stallion Last Chance, by Hunters Allen by Allan F-1 out of Merry Legs, also by Allan F-1.

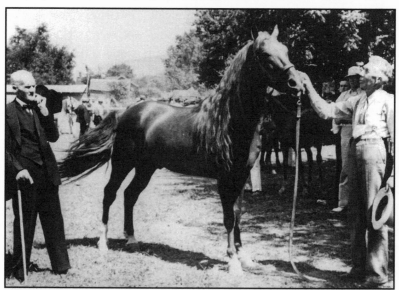

Photo courtesy of Harry Bosley

the Tennessee State Fair as a three year old. That day, the young horse won every class in which she was entered. After the show Dement was offered $950 for the mare, a very high price for a horse of that period. Dement declined the offer, later explaining that he "was dreaming of the future and refused to sell this mare. I had in mind a registered plantation stallion, and I felt that I had a foundation start with this mare." Dement couldn't have been more correct had he been gazing into a crystal ball.

On April 11, 1911 Nell Dement gave birth to Merry Legs—later designated Merry Legs F-4, the most influential broodmare in walking horse history. Besides being a great broodmare, Merry Legs herself was a top show ring contender. Henry Davis, another prominent breeder and trainer of Plantation Walking Horses, showed Merry Legs in 1911 as a weanling on a show circuit that included Murfreesboro, Tullahoma, Shelbyville, Winchester and Fayetteville, where she was undefeated. In 1913 Davis stopped by the Dement farm to pick up the as-yet unbroken filly for a show in Winchester, Tennessee. Davis spent a couple of days breaking Merry Legs to saddle before entering her in the show, where she took first place. That season she won every show on the circuit—despite the fact that her tail had been chewed off by calves to above the hocks.

Dement selectively bred Nell Dement and her daughter Merry Legs to outside Plantation stallions—his few attempts to use five-gaited saddle horses proved disappointing—and then to their own Plantation progeny. In this manner he produced a number of closely related individuals that he used extensively in his breeding program. It was the influence of this linebreeding program that eventually resulted in the development of the Tennessee Walking Horse.

Albert Dement's method of line breeding and inbreeding closely related individuals flew in the face of accepted breeding practices; at first many horse breeders had little faith that his methods would succeed. Dement himself, however, remained tenaciously dedicated to his vision of producing the Tennessee Walking Horse, a term he popularized. The area around Wartrace, Tennessee, where Dement was located, became known as the "Cradle" of the walking horse world, because of the many walking horses produced there. Besides Dement and several other large scale breeders, many of the area's small farms boasted one or two good walking horses that the owners used for breeding. Yankees came to this region in search of "one of those Tennessee Walking Horses."

Though the breed was called by many names, Albert Dement especially resisted calling the early walkers Plantation Saddle Horses, since that name linked them too closely to Louisiana, Mississippi, Alabama and Georgia, states that had many more large plantations than did Tennessee. Dement eventually began to use the term he heard from his many Yankee customers, and called his animals Tennessee Walking Horses.

As was the case for most utility animals during the 1910's, the market for Tennessee Walking Horses dried up at the same rate of speed that automobiles and farm machinery became popular. Thanks to the continued, often sacrificial, efforts of men like Albert Dement, Wartrace remained a repository for good walking horse blood and assured the breed's continuance. Often these men persevered in the face of great economic hardship and the catcalls of others.

OTHER IMPORTANT PEOPLE OF THE BREED

In the early 1920's the Tennessee Walking Horse regained popularity as a comfortable, stylish recreational animal. As the horse being produced around Wartrace became known as "The World's Greatest Pleasure Horse," it was inevitable that other breeders and trainers would spring up to help meet the increased demand for trained riding horses. Henry Davis was one such man, and served as a breeder, trainer, rider and prominent show horse judge of Tennessee Walking Horses for many years. Davis imported the stallion Giovanni (pronounced Go-van-e), a registered American Saddlebred, from Kentucky sometime around 1910. This famous stallion, who represents the last significant outcrossing of blood to the Tennessee Walking Horse, helped to improve and refine the conformation of the breed. Henry Davis is known as the "Father" of the famous annual Tennessee Walking Horse Celebration, a show held in Shelbyville, Tennessee ethe last ten days before Labor Day every year.

Floyd Carothers was Davis' partner in a large walking horse breeding operation in Wartrace for several years. Carothers gained a reputation for being an all time great Tennessee Walking Horse trainer and rider. James

Miller and Z.R. Pickens from Bell Buckle, Tennessee were two other successful trainers who worked in partnership. Pickens was a very large man, in excess of 250 pounds, but was nevertheless a superb professional horseman and rider. Pickens rode various horses to nine first place ribbons in the prestigious Stakes class at the Tennessee State Fair in Nashville during the 1920's and 30's.

Other men who must be mentioned in connection with the early breeding, training and successful promotion of the Tennessee Walking Horses include Steve Hill, Winston Wiser, Fred Walker and Bob Murchison. Later on a one-time state Senator by the name of Jimmie Joe Murray provided an important impetus for the continued success of the breed. He held a sale called the Murray Farm Sale at Lewisburg, Tennessee in 1938 which was to become a long-lived, annual event. In 1944 this walking horse enthusiast created the Murray Foundation for the purpose of promoting the Tennessee Walking Horse. The Murray foundation was active for seven years; the Murray Farm Sale in Lewisburg continues to be one of the nation's most important sources of quality walking horses.

Frank Barber began bringing walking horses into Louisiana around 1931. His promotional efforts resulted in such popularity for the breed around Baton Rouge, Louisiana that local government officials agreed to sponsor a walking horse show. Louisiana's Governor Leche was so enthusiastic about the project that he had a magnificent coliseum built at Louisiana State University to house the affair. The Baton Rouge Show, later to become known as the Dixie Jubilee, crowned the first World Grand Champion Tennessee Walking Horses (now that title is bestowed at the National Celebration in Shelbyville, Tennessee).

Besides breeders, trainers and promoters, the Tennessee Walking Horse has profited from the efforts of people who seem to have been nearly driven in their desire to accurately record the breed's bloodlines and history. Important breed genealogists and biographers include William J. McGill, Margaret Lindsley Warden, Ben A. Green and Dr. Bob Womack. Dr. Womack also wrote *The Echo of Hoofbeats*, the breed's authoritative history.

HEAVENLY GAITS

A BREED ASSOCIATION IS BORN

By the 1930's the Tennessee Walking Horse was gaining recognition, but there was as yet no official breed association. This changed on April 27, 1935, when a group of interested men gathered for the purpose of creating an association that would: *"...collect, record, and preserve the pedigrees of the strain of horses known as the Tennessee Walking Horse, wherever located; and the publication of a Register or Stud Book in such form as shall be adopted by the Association, and such other matters pertaining to the breeding, exhibiting, and sale of the strain of horses known as Tennessee Walking Horses, as may be deemed advisable."*

This organization was originally titled the Tennessee Walking Horse Breeder's Association of America. The "of America" was included so that people would associate the horse with breeders outside of Tennessee. In 1974 the Association's name was changed to The Tennessee Walking Horse Breeders' and Exhibitors' Association, to reflect interests of members who were interested in showing, but not necessarily breeding, Tennessee Walking Horses.

The first President of the Association was Burt Hunter; former Governor James McCord was named Secretary/Treasurer. These two men are believed to have been the main impetus behind the formation of the Association, and they each served two-year terms (1935-1937). A Mr. D.H. Brock served as President from 1937-1938. During these first four years after the Association's founding the number of registrations of Tennessee Walking Horses grew by leaps and bounds. The first year saw only 208 horses registered, but this changed dramatically once owners of these horses realized that out-of-state buyers preferred to purchase registered, pedigreed stock.

The horse's popularity coincided with a growing national economic prosperity fueled by the manufacture and sale of war materials for the Allies. This came right on the heels of the Great Depression, and people were eager to find ways to enjoy their new-found prosperity. The Murray Farm Sale held in Lewisburg in 1938 saw people buying Tennessee Walking Horses to take home to California, Montana, Illinois, Indiana, Texas, Louisiana, Alabama, North and South Carolinas, Georgia, Mississippi, Ohio, Pennsylvania and

Virginia. That same year Smyrna, Tennessee offered the first $500 Walking Horse Stake class, which drew people from many states. By 1939 the breed truly had become the Tennessee Walking Horse "of America."

The next four two-year Presidents of the Association were held by breed greats Albert Dement (1938-1940), Dr. W.F. Fessey (1940-1941), Henry Davis (1941-1943), and James Brantley's son, French Brantley (1943-1945). Under their astute management, the Association would see remarkable growth in the Tennessee Walking Horse industry.

THE NATIONAL CELEBRATION

In 1939 Henry Davis promoted the first Tennessee Walking Horse National Celebration in Shelbyville, Tennessee. The annual Celebration has since then become the highlight of the year, both for Middle Tennessee, and for the owners, breeders and trainers of Tennessee Walking Horses all over the nation.

By this time the visionary efforts of Albert Dement and other early breeders had paid off in the flesh a beautifully conformed, smooth walking horse who carried himself with dignity and pride. The beauty, versatility and gentle nature of these horses could hardly have had a better ambassador than Strolling Jim, the horse by Wilson's Allen who was crowned World Grand Champion in 1939, the first year of the National Celebration.

Appropriately enough, it was Henry Davis who discovered Strolling Jim. Davis himself one time related the story this way to breed historian Ben Green:

> "I happened by Charlie Ramsey, Jr.'s farm one day in the fall and he told me, 'I've got a little saddle horse that is one of the easiest riding horses you ever saw. I'll show him to you.'
>
> "Charlie brought out Strolling Jim, a gelding, and he looked like a bag of bones. The horse had been worked almost to death dragging a plow and other farm implements. I felt a great pity for the horse, because I could see he wasn't really built for that kind of work. So I told Charlie, 'Now you put up that horse. Feed him up and put some meat on his bones.'

"'I'll do it right now,' Charlie promised, and he did so.

"My mind often went back to this horse---because he showed real possibilities under that haggard appearance.

"Next spring I drove to Shelbyville one morning. Just as I got out of the car someone asked me 'Who are those strangers in town I heard were looking for a saddle horse?'

"My mind went back to Strolling Jim. I immediately returned to my car, put aside my business in town, and drove as fast as I could to Wartrace where I picked up Floyd Carothers. We hurried on to Charlie Ramsey's place and after a little talking I bought Jim for $350.

"We had closed the deal when up drove the two strangers with Charles Ramsey, Sr. The strangers wanted to buy the horse but would not pay me $100 more than I had paid for him. They offered just $25 more.

"I turned them down. They followed us and finally offered me $50 more, but I said that I had changed my mind and wouldn't sell him for $100 more. Strolling Jim went to our training barn in Wartrace, and Floyd Carothers rode him to the first Grand Championship of the World as a three-year-old less than six months later. He was an awful [awesome] horse."

Another gelded son of Wilson's Allen, Haynes Peacock, took the World Grand Championship title in Shelbyville in 1940 and 1941. This horse, who won the title as a thirteen year old, had never been shown until the previous spring, when he was entered in an impromptu, small-town show. Since the promoters of that event could ill afford to offer large prizes as incentives for people to bring their good horses to compete in the show, they decided to offer groceries. Haynes Peacock was crowned first place winner of the day—and won a bag of flour. Over the course of one year the proud Haynes Peacock, competing against horses one-third his age, rose from virtual obscurity to world-wide recognition.

These first two National World Champions were a prime example of the way Tennessee Walking Horses could "do it all—with style."

ASSOCIATION MEETS IMPORTANT CHALLENGES

Selection of individual horses to be designated Foundation Stock was rather a frustrating but important first item of business for the new Breeders' Association. Many of the horses known to have made significant contributions to the breed were long dead, their breeding and performing records scanty, unreliable or non-existent. Association members held differing bloodline loyalties, and there was a great deal of vehement discussion over whether the Hal or Allen horses should hold the most prominent positions—a disagreement that continued among breed historians for many years. Only with the wisdom afforded by hindsight can we now see clearly that the Association made the right choice when they gave Black Allan the title Allan F-1. After many months of research, and more than a few heated disagreements, the Breeders' Association chose 115 horses as Foundation Sires and Dams.

Though these horses were chosen early on, and the Tennessee Walking Horse Breeders' Association of America possessed a Tennessee state charter, the Association's challenges were not over. The Federal Government refused to recognize the Tennessee Walking Horse as a distinct breed. Not until 1947, after a twelve year effort by the Breeders' Association, did the government declare the Tennessee Walking Horse to be a "distinct and pure breed of light horse."

The Association faced many more challenges in its early years. In 1952 the Breeders' Board of Directors met and passed a regulation that prohibited the use of artificial insemination. This happened largely because too many people were using artificial insemination to get foals by Midnight Sun, which would in the long run have resulted in more inbreeding than Association officials believed was good. AI also made it difficult for other stallion owners to compete their horses against two-time World Champion Midnight Sun for stud services. By artificial means Midnight Sun was able to sire several hundred foals each year. This was perhaps a good financial situation for Wirt and Alex Harlan, who owned the stallion, but not so good for the rest of the Tennessee Walking Horse industry.

HEAVENLY GAITS

A "SORE" POINT

By the early fifties a new challenge faced the Tennessee Walking Horse. Greater emphasis was placed on breeding and training horses for the show ring. Crowds enthusiastically supported the show horses that demonstrated the greatest speed, lift and animation in their gaits. This type of horse became known as the "Big Lick" Tennessee Walking Horse.

The smooth, docile, low-moving Tennessee Walking horse, as designed by nature and wise breeders, was not as naturally high strung, fast and animated as his Saddlebred cousin. He had been bred to take his rider comfortably over muddy, rutted roads and fields, which requirement hardly called for great animation and speed. In an effort to produce a horse that would please the show audiences, trainers began selectively breeding for this new type of horse, and to institute training techniques and devices that further enhanced the Big Lick show ring performance.

Unfortunately, eager to show their horses to be the equal of any, and better than most, a new reign of trainers began to exaggerate the Big Lick action in their horses by applying chemical soring agents to the pasterns of their show horses. When boots were placed on the pastern over these chemicals the hide was quickly rubbed sore, which resulted in the horse lifting his front legs very quickly, and high, in an effort to keep his sore front feet off the ground. The resulting gait was dramatically changed from the original ground-covering running walk. But the sored, big-eyed Big Lick walking horses were so popular in the show ring that any breeder or trainer desiring to make or maintain a name for himself in the market during that period was nearly forced to practice soring his show horses to in order to compete with other sored horses. Though there were many trainers with integrity who protested the use of soring, their voices had little effect during the storm of popularity enjoyed by Big Lick walking horses.

Ironically, it was the spectators who demanded the flashy action brought about by the use of soring who eventually began to decry the inhumane aspects of the practice. The controversy surrounding this issue raised a cloud of dissension over the entire Tennessee Walking Horse world during the 50's and 60's.

To protect the interests of the breed, the State of Tennessee and the TWHBEA formulated rules forbidding the practice of soring horses and to ensure that training methods used to produce the Big Lick were ethical and not harmful to the horse. Unfortunately, enforcement of these regulations was inefficient. So in 1970 the U.S. Congress passed The Horse Protection Act in an effort to eliminate sored walking horses from the show rings of America. Enforcement of the act was administered by the United States Department of Agriculture.

From the industry side, the National Horse Show Regulatory Committee was formed to sanction horse shows and license responsible horse show judges. This Committee's name was later changed to the National Horse Show Commission, which agency still regulates the Tennessee Walking Horse show industry through self-policing policies. Tennessee Walking Horse owners and trainers now adhere to strict show ring guidelines, and must be willing to submit to pre-show and post-show examination of horses by the United States Department of Agriculture. This has at least decreased the number of sored horses entering Association-approved shows.

PLANTATION AND LITE-SHOD WALKING HORSES

Largely because of the controversy surrounding the practice of soring Big Lick horses, and the stress that the current Association wisely places on the versatility of the walking horse, most (90%) contemporary Tennessee Walking Horses are used without pads, boots or training devices. The popularity of, and number of show classes for, less heavily shod Plantation Walking Horses, as well as for lite shod horses, is increasing all the time.

Plantation Walking Horses are shown without pads, weights or other artificial training or action devices. Plantation shoes must not exceed 1/2" in thickness or 1-1/2" in width, and the heel of the shoe cannot extend beyond the bulbs of the feet. Caulks are allowed, but the thickness of the shoe and caulk together must not exceed 1-1/8". While the Plantation shoe is heavier than an everyday horse shoe, it is nevertheless a more humane way to encourage more show ring action and style. Because of the wide-spread, growing interest in these kinds of horses, there is now a separate registry for

HEAVENLY GAITS

Plantation Walking Horses.

The lite shod Tennessee Walking Horse is also making a come-back. As the name suggests, these horses wear shoes that are smaller and lighter than either the Big Lick or Plantation style of shoe. TWHBEA rules for lite shod classes dictate a shoe no wider than 3/4" or more than 3/8" thick. As with Plantation shoes, heel caulk and shoe thickness may not exceed 1-1/8".

These kinds of walking horses often make excellent hunter/jumpers, can be driven, are sure-footed, and have great endurance and stamina. Best of all, the Tennessee Walking Horse—long known as "The World's Greatest Pleasure Horse"—is more and more being bred by responsible people for its gentle temperament and the comfortable, low-slung running walk that made it the toast of a nation.

PHYSICAL CHARACTERISTICS OF THE TWH

The Tennessee Walking Horse sports the full range of colors, excepting Appaloosa spot patterns (though there is a separate registry for the half-bred Tennessee Walking Horse/Appaloosa). Chestnut, black and sorrel are the three most common colors. Roan used to be prevalent, but declined in popularity during the sixties and seventies. As with many other breeds, there's currently a renewed interest in breeding for color, so pinto, palomino and roan walking horses are more common than they were a decade ago.

This breed of horse typically stands between 15 and 16 hands. His head has a noble appearance, with a straight profile and a notably round, prominent and expressive eye. The ears of the walking horse are large in comparison with other breeds, but always in good proportion to the rest of the head. His gracefully arched, medium length neck connects smoothly into the top of well-defined withers. The back may be medium or short in length, but either way should be well coupled to smooth and substantially muscled hindquarters. Tennessee Walkers have broad, well-muscled chests and deep heart girths. Their legs boast excellent but refined bone and well-defined joints. The back legs of most walking horses are well angled, as are the pelvis, shoulder, and pastern joints. The foot is substantial.

The mane of a Tennessee Walker is flowing and long. Usually the bridle path is clipped back one ear's length, and he appears in the show ring with ribbons braided into his forelock and top mane. He has a long waterspout tail that is proudly carried up and out, like a banner.

USING THE TENNESSEE WALKING HORSE

The average person can easily learn to ride and handle a well-bred Tennessee Walking Horse for any type of light horse use. While walkers often

Today's Tennessee Walking Horses, and their owners, are defying the old stereotypes about the breed. An increasing number are spotted, lite or plantation shod, and ridden in traditional western style. Below, Lisa Hamilton on Slick Chick.

Photo by Mickey Anderson

HEAVENLY GAITS

are spirited in their way of going, and are fast moving, they usually possess even, willing and sensible temp .aments. The typical walking horse has a bright, eager and sweet expression, and seldom shies or acts unpredictable. These animals genuinely enjoy their association with people, and rarely look for ways to duck out of work.

THE WALKING HORSE GAIT

Unfortunately, modern walking horse stock still reflect the strong pacing blood that was bred so strongly into the Big Lick Walkers during the 1950's and 60's. Though a tendency to pace is essential to the breeding of a good walking horse, this can sometimes become too heavy an influence, especially for a horse intended for everyday, flat-shod use. Such a horse may

The stallion Sin's Peter Piper, owned and ridden here by Eleanor Hultbert, demonstrates the long-strided running walk. Though humane device may enhance the horse's natural show gait, horses not naturally gaited will never show this kind of form, regardless of devices or training methods.

Photo couresy of Sharon Major, Horsetrend Magazine

be rough-gaited at the walk, and unbalanced at the canter. Those people desiring a truly smooth, versatile horse with a good running walk must do their homework well, and choose a horse that has been bred for lite-shod use by a knowledgeable breeder.

Such a horse maintains the smooth gaits that makes this breed so popular. Besides the flat walk and a smooth, rolling "rocking chair" canter, the Tennessee Walking Horse is famed for his smooth, gliding, ground-covering running walk. This unique gait is a natural inborn characteristic of the breed. While it's possible to improve the gait of a horse that is too trotty or pacey, a true running walk cannot be trained in, but must be inherited.

A good running walk is a true, square, evenly-timed four-beat gait. Except for the exaggerated head nod and deeper action of the hind legs, it is similar to the rack, with each foot picking up and setting down independently.

REINFORCING THE NATURAL RUNNING WALK

Horses who possess the running walk may need some encouragement to perform it, or to perform it well. There are methods that help the owner of such a mount to deal with common gait problems without the assistance of a professional horse trainer. Since the walking horse is generally intelligent and has an even temperament, seldom will the owner of one of these horses need to resort to drastic or harsh training measures. Knowledge and patience are the walking horse owner's most effective training tools.

A young horse is ready to perform his gait under the weight of a rider after he has been accustomed to the snaffle bridle, and to performing simple figure eights and other suppling and back-strengthening work at the walk under saddle. A shanked curb or mullen-mouth bit is used once the horse is bridle wise and ready to go on to more advanced training. The weight and balance of a good walking horse bit helps the horse to use his head and neck properly, which in turn enables him to carry and move his body in proper form. Such a bit, however, requires good hands. If a rider is even slightly insecure in the saddle, then he or she should stick to mild jointed snaffle bits, and get a trainer to "set in" the horse's gait.

The kind of saddle used is up to the rider. Though walkers are commonly ridden in flat saddle-seat saddles, they readily adapt to hunt seat, western or Australian style saddles. What's more important than saddle style is that the saddle fit the horse, and be comfortable for the rider. The horse needs complete freedom of motion in the shoulders, which are usually laid well back. So it is important to check that the tree of the saddle settles behind, rather than on top of, the horse's shoulder blade. This may especially be a problem with some very short-backed walking horses, so the fit of such tack must be checked carefully.

To encourage the greenbroke horse to perform his gait, he is worked at a flat walk over level ground for many weeks. Once he's well balanced and loose at the flat walk, the rider begins, on a straightaway, to ask for more speed while driving him into the bit. While the rider's hands are still giving to the motion of his head, he's maintaining more tension on the reins. When the horse first starts to demonstrate the pleasurable, gliding running walk, the temptation is often to immediately ask for more speed—but that's a mistake. A horse pushed to perform the gait too fast, too soon, will be unable to do so; to try to please his rider he will almost surely drop out of form. Such a hurried horse begins to pace, amble, trot or fox trot, depending upon his inclinations. A person inexperienced with the gait may not be able to differentiate between the running walk and the amble or fox-trot, which will result in the horse learning an incorrect way of going. While there's nothing inherently wrong with the fox-trot or amble as a simple way of going—quite the contrary, as both are comfortable gaits—many walking horse fans insist they should be properly taught to perform the unique gait for which they were bred.

Once the horse is moving along with a good nod to the head and long reaching strides, the good walking horse trainer/rider maintains that speed. As the horse becomes accustomed to working at the running walk, he will naturally develop more speed. Most non-gaited horses ridden with a well-trained walker have to jog right along to keep up. This is generally a good rule of thumb for those who wonder how fast a good natural running walk should be: a good running walk approximates the speed of a slow jog-trot. This is fast enough for most pleasure riders, especially considering that the Tennessee Walking Horse's gait is incredibly sure-footed and comfortable. If a rider wants something faster, he can always ask for a canter.

SOLVING GAIT PROBLEMS

Some horses have been poorly trained and/or ridden and subsequently mixed up their gaits. Others who have been bred with a preponderance of trotting or pacing blood need encouragement to move in good form. Whatever the cause, a horse that doesn't perform a good running walk can usually be taught to take up, and/or improve, his natural gait.

A horse that tends to pace can be very challenging. Such horses often become slab sided. It is then the rider's job to condition the horse so that his body becomes rounded and supple, which will greatly enhance his ability to perform the running walk.

To do this, the horse is longed at the walk in a twenty to thirty foot circle, in both directions, every day for a week or ten days. Then he is lunged at the walk over cavaletti, also in both directions. Requiring him to pick up his feet a bit higher to clear the cavaletti forces him to fold his knees higher and break up the extreme forward action of the pace. At no time should the trainer allow the horse to break into a pace. When he slips into that gait, the trainer may say "Quit!", step toward his head, and shake the lunge line to slow him down. If this causes the horse to get too excited, he may be stopped altogether, calmed with a few quiet words, and started over at the walk. While ground-work progresses, work under saddle also continues. The horse should be ridden for many hours at the flat walk, and perhaps for an hour or so every day in small circles and spirals in a collected flat walk.

After two or three weeks of such work, the horse is a great deal stronger and more supple, and ready to perform his natural running walk. The rider simply pushes the horse on from the flat walk to a faster speed, and anytime he slips into a pace, stepping pace (amble) or rack (no nod, no overstride), he is checked by the rider. Though many of us *love* to ride an ambling or racking horse, at this stage of training the walking horse must only be allowed to *walk* so that he comes to understand clearly what is expected of him.

A common and useful method to firmly establish a running walk is to work the animal over newly plowed fields, uneven ground, or through deep grass. Working on an uphill slant also helps (though downhill work encourages the pace, and is therefore kept to a minimum). Each of these situations encourages the horse to reach deeply underneath his body with his hind feet. The rider will know the horse has hit his running walk stride when his head starts nodding vigorously in time to a reaching, rolling four-beat lick.

An occasional horse is so determined to pace that he requires additional help from a farrier, who will want to "square him up". Sometimes this is accomplished by slightly lowering the angle of the hind heel while shortening the front toe for a faster breakover. Exceptionally strong pacers may require heavier "plantation" shoes to break up the rhythm of the pace. Remedies are varied, and what works for one horse might not work for another. Ask other walking horse and gaited horse riders from your area for the name of a farrier who can help you sort out gait problems. Preferably you'll work with someone who will attempt to get your horse to perform his best quality gait using the least amount of artificial manipulation.

A word here about farriers: they can be the gaited horse owner's best friend, or worst enemy. A good farrier will work closely with both owner and horse, and make moderate adjustments until consistently good results are achieved. The owner who finds such a treasure should continue to use that person's services even if he or she charges more than another farrier might. Farrier work that is merely convenient and/or cheap may prove in the long run to be both time-consuming and expensive.

Sometimes a horse prefers the trot or fox-trot to the running walk. Such a horse must be ridden many long miles to loosen up at the flat walk. Once he's very loose and relaxed, he is gradually pushed into the running walk —he is *never* allowed to trot. Since downhill work encourages lateral gaits, working such a horse over slightly declining ground also helps. This training sometimes takes several weeks, and again, a farrier's assistance may be needed.

THE CANTER

The canter is a natural, easy gait for the well bred walking horse to perform under saddle. Once in awhile, however, we see particularly pacey horses who prefer a fast pace to the canter. Such horses may have difficulty learning to canter. They either cross canter (take opposite leads fore and hind), or do a leaping canter, where the horse leaps back and forth from his front legs to his hind. Either action is unacceptable.

The cross-cantering horse risks hitting a front leg with a back foot, which is known as interference. This can cause him to seriously injure a leg, or to trip on his own foot and fall. A cross canter is terrible to ride—it feels like you're sitting on top of a spring that keeps bouncing you forcefully up into the air. Like the cross-canter, the leaping canter is unbalanced, uncomfortable and unsafe. It can cause a horse to fall forward into a somersault, to twist a front leg, or to seriously strain muscles and ligaments. Every time the horse leaps forward the rider is pushed forcefully from the saddle.

Before trying to teach a horse to canter properly, his body is conditioned and suppled by working him at the flat walk in ever decreasing sized figure eights, spirals and circles for three or four weeks. Once he's well conditioned and supple, it is common to begin canter work on the side of a hill. One method sometimes employed entails taking the horse to a hillside trail with another, well-trained, horse. At the foot of the hill the other rider cues his horse to canter. The problem horse usually tries to go leaping and longeing after the other horse—but is held back for a beat or two while natural gravity causes his weight to shift backward. Thus a simple law of physics is used to collect the horse so he can properly spring forward from his hind quarters. Just as the horse achieves good strong collection (and before he leaps forward wildly) his head is subtly reined to one side while he is cued behind the girth on the opposite side, signalling the correct canter lead. The rider also leans slightly forward and avoids a too-tight rein.

Few horses will canter improperly given the above set of circumstances. Once a good canter is established, is maintained for as long as possible. Ideally it can be maintained after horse and rider reach flat ground. If it is not, the horse is brought back to a walk, and the exercise is repeated at each hill or slight incline until the horse canters correctly even on flat ground. This may take several days of consistent work. Once such horses are sufficiently conditioned mentally and physically to perform a strong, balanced canter, they rarely cause further trouble. He will have developed the right kind of "muscle memory" to keep on doing the job correctly.

Particularly pacey horses who need to be worked like this to improve their gaits can become perfectly acceptable riding horses. Indeed, a tendency for lateral action is essential to the production of good walking horse gaits. But where such breeding has been overdone in an effort to enhance the Big Lick, it has created the above kinds of gait problems in lite-shod horses. Such horses, if used for breeding, must be conscientiously bred to horses whose contribution will strengthen the natural gaits of the Tennessee Walking Horse. (This means breeding to a trottier-type of horse.)

TENNESSEE WALKING HORSE SHOWS AND SALES

There are currently over a quarter of a million Tennessee Walking Horses registered with the TWHBEA. These are scattered mostly throughout the United States, though recently a great deal of interest in the horse has been shown by people from Canada, Mexico and several European nations.

Tennessee Walking Horses can be purchased at any number of breeding establishments throughout the country, of course. But it's always fun to attend the big sales that specialize in this breed. Besides the Murray Farm Sale, the Harlinsdale Farm breeding program sponsors the C.A. Bobo

The Tennessee Walking Horse can use its smooth, long stride under harness as well as under saddle. Here Flashing Sundance shows off the excellent form that helped him win the Mid-Atlantic Pleasure Driving Division. Owner/Driver is Jack Mauzy; trainer Jeff Hatcher.

Photo courtesy of TWHBEA

Lillian Reames Burnett takes Mighty Copy LL through a barrel racing pattern, showing the breed to be as athletic as any other. This 1988 TWH was National High Point Champion walking horse in Barrels, Poles, and Water Glass competitions.

Sellabration Sale each year during the last four days of the Celebration. At any time during the National Celebration visitors to Shelbyville and the surrounding areas will discover a host of yearling sales being held.

The National Celebration in Shelbyville, Tennessee remains the largest Tennessee Walking Horse show in the world, and offers classes for every type, sex and age of Walking Horse. The Dixie Jubilee in Baton Rouge, Louisiana is still an important walking horse show. The Walking Horse Trainers' Association hosts an annual National Trainers' Show at various locations throughout the Southeast, which is usually the region's first major show of the season. A Spring Fun Show is held at the Calsonic Arena on the Celebration grounds in Shelbyville each year during the three days (Thursday - Saturday) prior to the Memorial Day holiday. The Walking Horse Owners' Association sponsors the International Championship Walking Horse Show in Murfreesboro, Tennessee during the first week of August each year. This show offers over 140 classes for all types of walking horses. The TWHBEA sponsors an annual futurity for weanlings, yearlings, two and three year old Tennessee Walking Horses who have been nominated for the futurity, with paid fees. The Western States Celebration—open to walking horses as well as Missouri Fox Trotters—is held each Mid-October in Reno, Nevada.

Other shows with walking horse classes are held in virtually every region of every state in the nation. The Tennessee Walking Horse may also be competed in any other type of show class as well, as long as the judge is informed in advance that the horse performs the running walk as an intermediate gait, in lieu of the jog or trot.

A person desiring to compete a walker under such circumstances need not feel apologetic or out of place. Wherever the Tennessee Walking Horse makes an appearance, he garners the attention and admiration of people who appreciate the qualities of a truly outstanding horse.

Photo by Mickey Anderson

—Chapter Four—
The Missouri Fox Trotting Horse

The Missouri Fox Trotter's story is a tale of ordinary, hard working people who produced an extraordinary horse. From the time Missouri gained statehood in 1821 until the present, one of the state's main industries has been the raising of cattle. The development of the Missouri Fox Trotter came about largely because of the special requirements of the rugged cattlemen who lived on widely scattered farms in the hills and hollows of the rocky, densely forested Ozark Mountains of Missouri. These men used their horses to drive herds of cattle—sometimes very large herds—over long distances and hard-to navigate terrain. They needed mounts who were extremely hardy, sure-footed and fast. They also had to possess a lot of "cow sense." Since these cattlemen often spent weeks at a time in the saddle, comfortable saddle gaits were essential. Over time it became evident to these men that horses who naturally performed the easy-to-sit fox trot were particularly adept at maneuvering over rough trails, and they began to breed horses for that gait.

Missouri has long been known as a southern state that boasts excellent horses. Many of the nation's most prominent early horse breeders and trainers—and top gaited horse bloodstock—were located in the northern part of Missouri. During the mid-1800's Mexico, Missouri was especially famed for its wealth of Saddle Horses and Saddle Horse trainers, while in 1893 Kansas City, Missouri hosted the first Royal Horse Show. Since the state—and the nearby southern states of Virginia, Kentucky and Tennessee—possessed so much excellent horse stock, it was perhaps to be expected that Ozark area

Photo by Bert Simpson, courtesy of Terex Images

Missouri Fox Trotters were developed and used by cattlemen of the Ozarks, and still retain a talent for working cattle. Above, Missouri Fox Trotter Willard and owner/rider Rex Walker learn how to rope together.

cattlemen would utilize these horses to produce a unique breed of gaited horse all their own. And that's exactly what they did.

EARLY HISTORY OF THE BREED

Most of the horses originally brought into the Missouri Ozarks carried a heavy influence of Saddle Horse breeding, with a sprinkling of genes from other light horse sources—particularly the influence of the Canadian Pacer, Tom Hal, and the Morgan horse. Prior to the civil war, racing was a popular pastime in the Ozarks, as it was throughout most of America. Certain families of the region became known for their fast racing stock. The Alsups were one such family, and their most important sire and race horse was named Bremmer. Bremmer sired many excellent prepotent sons and daughters, most of which became known for speed as well as smooth saddle gaits. From the Bremmer line of horses came other famous Missouri Fox Trotting horses.

Daniel Bouray on H.E. Punado, a Missouri Fox Trotter. Fox trotters are sure-footed and quick over difficult hilly or mountainous terrain.

Another Ozark family noted for their good horses were the Kissees. They developed the horses Old Fox and Old Diamond. Many of the farming families of that region and era could afford only one good horse—to own a horse from one of these lines gave the family great prestige in the community. The names of these horses still appear on the pedigrees of famous Missouri Fox Trotters.

It has been claimed by some that early fox trotters were developed using horses possessing the blood of the Bullets, Copperbottoms, Steel Dusts, Cold Decks, Chiefs, Kentucky Whips, Kentucky Hickory, Hickory Boys, Sea Foams, and others—though this is disputed by some breed authorities, who make the point that none of these names has ever appeared on a Missouri Fox Trotting Horse's pedigree. What is undisputed is the influence made by the Canadian Pacer Tom Hal. Tom Hal horses were highly valued and used extensively by Missouri Fox Trotter breeders—as they were by breeders of Tennessee Walking Horses, Saddle Horses and Standardbreds.

Individual horses who had a direct influence on the early breeding of fox trotting horses were Old Charley, Deacon, Betty Fox, Nan, Lady, Ted, and Dusty (F-176). Ted and Dusty were stallions who became especially noted for siring excellent mares. Both of them sired three daughters who produced World Champion Missouri Fox Trotters. Dusty's record might eventually have surpassed Ted's, had the popular Palomino stallion not died of colic at seven years of age.

The development of fox trotters in the early part of this century was facilitated by Missouri cattlemen who converged regularly at the stockyards. These occasions gave them the opportunity to see and evaluate one another's horses, and arrange for sales, trades and breedings. Often, stallions from particular regions gained reputations as good sires and were used extensively, and exclusively, by people in that region. In other words, horse breeding depended much upon whether two horses happened to cross paths, or be from the same region, or "hollow." In fact, though breeders of fox trotters eventually became more sophisticated in their selections and breeding practices, it long remained common practice to use stallions simply because they were located near the mare. As late as the 1940's Golden Governor—the breed's most influential foundation sire—was born, used as stud, and died within a two-mile area in Laclede County, Missouri. (Though the second of his two owners did take the popular stallion to parades and shows in other parts of Missouri). These circumstances don't negate the skill that went into early breeding; on the contrary, the breeders in question were excellent judges of horse flesh, knew precisely what kind of horse they wanted to produce, and succeeded in doing so despite limiting circumstances.

In the early 1930's bloodstock from Middle Tennessee's Plantation Walking Horse began to be utilized by breeders of fox trotters, who discovered that this breeding helped to extend and improve the fox trotter's flat walk. Walking Horse crosses soon became so popular that many of the Missouri Fox Trotter's finest modern day representatives carry heavy infusions of blood from such famous Tennessee Walking horses as Allan F-1, Roan Allen, Wilson's Allen, Merry Legs, Merry Boy, Midnight Sun, Panola, Ramsey's Rena, Wiser's Dimples, Last Chance, and others. Also at about this time, like Plantation Walking Horse and Saddle Horse breeders, fox trotting enthusiasts began line-breeding, and inbreeding, their best bloodstock.

Saddlebred sires also made significant contributions to the Missouri Fox Trotter. Chester Dare and Rex McDonald are two famous Saddlebred sires who are known to be progenitors of important Missouri Fox Trotting Horses. Chester Dare appears in the pedigree of the famous Missouri Fox Trotter mare Nancy Ann. Rex McDonald was great-great grand sire to a Wheeler McCain fox trotting mare known as Betty Fox. Betty Fox was the dam of Golden Governor, three-time producer of World Champion Missouri Fox

Trotting Horses (Lucky Strike, 1962; Red Warrior, 1964; and Golden Rawhide, 1966).

GOLDEN GOVERNOR

Golden Governor's breeder and original owner was Joe McCain, though Joe's father, Wheeler McCain, always managed the stallion. Tragedy struck the Wheeler family twice in a three year period. Joe McCain died in an automobile accident in 1951 at the age of 39, and then his father, Wheeler McCain, died in 1954. One of the Wheeler's long-time neighbors, Walter Esther, had always expressed interest in Golden Governor, who was never for sale so long as Joe and Wheeler McCain were alive. But in 1951 Walter Esther had also passed on.

Wheeler McCain's widow sold Golden Governor to Dale Esther, Walter's son, who bred his father's favorite fox trotter mare, Nancy Ann (the mare who traced to Chester Dare, who in turn traced to Tom Hal), to Golden Governor. This fortunate match resulted in a copper Palomino stud colt that Esther named Golden Rawhide. In 1966, Golden Rawhide was the first stallion to earn the Missouri Fox Trotting title of World Grand Champion in the MFTHBA's annual Celebration Show's seven year history. Despite Dale Esther's continued efforts to breed more good horses out of Nancy Ann, she proved to be a hard mare to settle. The only other foal she produced—also by Golden Governor—was Lady Anne, who became dam to Zane Grey, the modern breed's most significant and prepotent sire.

ZANE GREY

Zane Grey took the World Championship title at the Celebration in 1968, but as prestigious as that competition was, and is, that show ring victory was perhaps the least of the great stallion's accomplishments. Zane Grey's most significant contributions to the Missouri Fox Trotter came through his outstanding sons. When we look back at this stallion's history, it becomes easy to see the makings for greatness.

Zane Grey's sire was Sterling Merry Boy, a stallion who remains rather an enigma. He sired two World Grand Champion Missouri Fox Trotters (Zane Grey, 1968; and Starlight W., 1970) and became the grand sire or great grand sire to several others. Yet Sterling Merry Boy was never performance registered, and no one ever recalls seeing him under saddle. We do know however that Sterling Merry Boy boasted Tennessee Walking Horse blood tracing back on his sire's side to Wilson Allen and Byron Allen, and twice to Merry Boy on his dam's.

Zane Grey's dam, Lady Anne, was equally an equine "blue-blood," with maternal lines from Nancy Ann tracing back to Chester Dare, a Saddle Horse sire who was prominent during an era when the fox trot was still an acceptable show ring saddle gait. Lady Anne's sire, Golden Governor, was by Ozark Golden King and out of the mare Betty Fox. Ozark Golden King, besides siring Golden Governor, was grand sire to Sandy, the 1960 MFTHBA World Grand Champion. Betty Fox traced back to Rex McDonald. So from among his various family lines Zane Grey blended blood from such great horses as Allen F-1, Chester Dare, Rex McDonald, Ozark Golden King and Golden Governor. During his short life-span, Zane Grey amply proved the horseman's adage that "good blood wins out."

Zane's first colt was Diamond Duke, out of Diamond Head, herself the first foal sired by 1966 Grand Champion Golden Rawhide. Diamond Duke grew up to become the 1971 MFTHA's World Grand Champion.

The 1975 Missouri Fox Trotting Horse Breed Association's Celebration show in Ava, Missouri saw Pride of Princess S. and Zane's Charming Lad, two full brothers by Zane Grey, out of Princess S., battling for supremacy. By the time the Grand Championship class rolled around, four-year-old Pride of Princess S. had already been beaten for the blue in the Senior Stallion Performance Class by his older brother, Zane's Charming Lad. But during the Celebration's most important class, four-year-old Pride of Princess S. rose spectacularly to the occasion to garner the title World Grand Champion, while Zane's Charming Lad took Reserve Grand Champion. Tragically, this was the last show ring victory for Pride of Princess S., as the magnificent gray stallion died of colic two weeks later. Zane's Charming Lad, however, went on to prove himself a sire of outstanding horses. Listed among his get is the 1979 World Grand Champion mare, Zane's Charming Lady.

Zane Grey's most significant son was a product of mating the great stallion with his own champion-producing dam, Lady Anne. The resulting foal was Missouri Traveler E, the sire of three World Grand Champions (Travelin' Suzi, 1982; Missouri Red Wing, 1988; and Missouri's Bobbie Sue, 1989). In all, Zane Grey's name is listed more than a dozen times in the pedigrees of World Grand Champions, as well as many other top show ring contenders. This feat becomes especially noteworthy considering Zane Grey's relatively short life-span—he died 45 days short of his ninth year.

MIDNIGHT MACK K III

Another Missouri Fox Trotter sire who made significant contributions to modern World Champion breeding is Midnight Mack K. III, by Midnight Sun and out of Panola, two famed Tennessee Walking Horses. Midnight Mack K. III is the grand sire of Firepower, the 1978 World Grand Champion. More significantly, he is sire to Mack K's Yankee, sire of three World Grand Champions (Yankee's Mona Lisa, 1973; Yankee's Whispering Hope, 1981; and Yankee's Sweet Charity, 1983).

MISSOURI FOX TROTTING HORSE BREED ASSOCIATION

By 1948 breeders of the Missouri Fox Trotter were keenly interested in preserving the breeding of their unique horse. Fifteen of these men secured a charter for a breed organization, and began a stud book. These charter members were G.E. Dye, C.S. Neiman, Ralph Kerr, Homer Harley, E.L. Hesterlee, Paul Comer, Ranse Gaston, Clyde Norman, Ernest Uhlmann, C.H. Hibbard, John Dunn, Granville Prock, Ovle House, and Paul David. Their attorney was Bernie Lewis, and the new association was located in Ava, Missouri.

By 1955 several dozen horses—a precise figure has never been determined—had been registered with the association. But the charter suffered a major setback that year when a fire engulfed the Secretary's home, destroying the stud book and all of the records. Following this the organization floundered for several years until, in 1958, it was reorganized as a stock company by a larger group of people. The first 100 registration numbers were reserved for horses who had been granted registration papers before the original records were destroyed.

MFTHBA'S ANNUAL SHOW AND CELEBRATION

On Saturday, September 26, 1959, the newly reorganized Missouri Fox Trotting Horse Breed Association oversaw their first Celebration show, which was held on the baseball diamond in Ava, Missouri. That first show boasted a total of 14 classes, eight model classes and six performance classes. Since there was no open stakes class, a World Grand Champion was not named. Golden Governor, however, took first place blue in the Senior Performance Stallion class. Many of the horses entered in that first Celebration were examined and approved for registration just prior to their classes.

In fact, foundation stock could be examined and approved for registry with the MFTBA until 1982, when it became a requirement that at least one parent of a registered horse be a registered Missouri Fox Trotter. Starting in 1983, the association's books were closed, so that to be eligible for registration, foals had to be the product of two registered parents. Though the association was consistently strict about judging which horses were eligible for registry, the long-time open book policy of the MFTBA allowed fox trotters to outcross to outstanding horses of other breeds, thus expanding the breed's genetic pool, and guaranteeing that it remain an extremely versatile horse.

In 1977 the Celebration—with an expanded show schedule—was held at new show ground facilities that the MFTBA had purchased and developed just outside of Ava, Missouri. The annual Celebration is still held on these grounds every year, on Labor Day Weekend.

PROMINENT RIDERS AND TRAINERS

As is often the case, certain trainers began early on to make a name for themselves at the annual Celebration. One of the first trainers to do so was Paul Thompson, of West Plains, Missouri. Thompson rode three horses to the title of World Grand Champion: Sonny Man in 1961; Golden Rawhide in

1966; and Danney Joe W. in 1967.

Dale Esther, the breeder who oversaw the inspired match between Golden Governor and Nancy Ann—as well as many others over the years—himself rode Zane Grey to the World Grand Championship in 1968.

A trainer by the name of Jerry Middleton has ridden five horses to the prestigious title: Gold Bug in 1969; Zane's Charming Lady in 1979; Warrior's Gentleman Jim in 1980; Bo's April Charm in 1984; and Sensation's Gunsmoke in 1987. The Middleton family shares in this winning tradition, as Jerry's father Quentin won the World Grand Championship on Zane's Queen of Hearts in 1977. Geno Middleton, Jerry's son and Quentin's grandson, took his first World Grand Championship ride on Madam Sensation in 1986. At 18 years of age, he was the youngest rider to ever win the prestigious title. In 1989 Geno proved his first World Championship ride was more than beginner's luck by taking another one on Missouri's Bobbie Sue.

The Dampier family also have multi-generational World Grand Championship rides to their credit. Charlotte Dampier was the first woman to ride a horse to the title, and she did so in 1973 on Yankee's Mona Lisa, a mare that she raised, trained and showed herself. She repeated this feat in 1983 on Yankee's Sweet Charity.

Two other Dampiers—related to Charlotte's husband, L.D. Dampier—have visited the World Grand Champion winners circle. In 1988 Steve Dampier rode Missouri Red Wing to the Grand Champion stake title, and then took Rex's Golden Touch to the same victory in 1990. The Dampier tradition continues, as Justin Dampier, Steve's father, took Lady's Red Ruby J. to the World Grand Champion blue ribbon in 1991.

In 1974, just one year after Charlotte first demonstrated that a woman rider could win the Grand Championship stakes class, Janet Burks rode Mr. Red Jet to the title. She also earned the prestigious victory wreath for Firepower in 1978.

Other riders to have enjoyed the World Grand Championship winner's circle more than once are Dwight Sutherland (on Pride of Princess S. in 1975 and President's Mr. Jack in 1976); and Billy Johnson (on Yankee's Whispering Hope in 1981 and Black Cloud C. in 1985).

HEAVENLY GAITS

USES OF THE MISSOURI FOX TROTTER

It should be kept in mind that despite their fine appearance in the show ring, this breed of horse is still kept by most owners as a using horse. Of those horses who are shown, many are also enjoyed as everyday family or sports mounts. A perceptive person might notice, upon perusing through victory photographs taken at the Celebration in Ava, Missouri, that many of the owners of these horses do not appear especially glamorous or wealthy. People attracted to this breed are often ordinary horse-loving people who appreciate the talented Missouri Fox Trotting horse for his easy, sure-footed gaits, extraordinary good sense, intelligence, good looks, athletic abilities, and kind temperament.

These qualities enable the Missouri Fox Trotter to be used in a wide variety of pursuits. They are such superb trail and pack horses that the U.S. Forest Service uses more than 1,000 Missouri Fox Trotters as rangers' mounts. They also have become a popular choice for competitive and endurance trail riders. Their proud carriage and non-spooky nature make them excellent parade horses, and they retain a talent for working cattle. One would be hard put to discover a horse-related pastime at which the Missouri Fox Trotter fails to excel. These horses are as much at home traversing rough mountain ranges and carrying children through pastures as they are exhibiting at the spectacular Celebration show grounds in Ava, Missouri.

PHYSICAL CHARACTERISTICS OF THE MFTH

The Missouri Fox Trotting Horse stands between 14 and 16 hands in height, and is very well muscled. He carries an attractive, refined head with a tapered muzzle atop a medium-length neck. The neck is set high on sloping shoulders and well-defined withers. His ears are medium length, alert and pointed. The fox trotter's back is short, and tightly coupled to well-muscled flank and loins. His ribs are deep and well-spring, his chest muscular. He has a long, abundant mane and tail. Good-sized, tough feet are topped by tapered, well-muscled legs that exhibit substantial bone and scope of movement.

Photo by Terex Images

A sturdy, yet refined appearance is the hallmark of a well-conformed Missouri Fox Trotting Horse.

Because of the genetic diversity of this breed, The Missouri Fox Trotter sports nearly every color known to horsedom including black, bay, brown, chestnut, gray, dun, buckskin, sorrel, roan and spotted. During the 1940's it became popular practice to breed for palomino coloring, and this usually rare coloration is not uncommon among fox trotters today.

SHOWING THE MISSOURI FOX TROTTER

Unlike the American Saddlebred and the Tennessee Walking Horse, The Missouri Fox Trotter is most often shown under western tack, with a colored browband/cavesson bridle and western bit. Riders wear western style attire. Colorful ribbons are braided into the horse's forelock and top of mane.

117

The ridden horse should travel straight with a four-beat fox trot rhythm, long reaching strides, and an elevated head and tail. His tail may bob and his head should nod in time to the rhythm of his gait---some of these horses nod so vigorously that their teeth can be heard clacking with every stride!

Fox trotters are shown at the walk, fox trot, and canter. The flat walk is performed at speeds of 3-4 miles per hour, with long strides and animation. The fox trot gait is a broken 4-beat diagonal gait, with the front foot landing ahead of the diagonally opposed hind foot and the back foot disfiguring or overstepping the print of the front foot. The back foot tends to slide in under the horse, rather than striking hard and flat on the ground. The fox trotting horse has two or three feet on the ground at all times. The ideal show ring canter is a moderately collected gait performed with some contact on the bit. It should be neither too high and animated, nor too low and uncollected.

Fox trotters are shown with plain keg shoes—weights, pads and other artificial devices are strictly forbidden, as is the practice of soring horses. Running martingales, tie-downs, chains, rollers and tail sets are also prohibited. Whips and spurs are permitted.

Though designed as a practical "using" horse, the Missouri Fox Trotter can be as stylish as the best show horse. Below, Denise Darr rides sidesaddle on Mr. Jack's Gambler, a MFT owned by Jim Hufft, Marshfield, MO.

Photo courtesy of Favorite Gait magazine

RIDING AND TRAINING THE MISSOURI FOX TROTTER

Riding a fox trotter is well within the scope of most people, even novices, as he is smooth to sit and generally has a very even, eager-to-please temperament. The rider should sit deep in the saddle and keep the horse moderately collected while using leg and seat aids to ask the horse to extend his stride. Moderate contact with the bit must be maintained, which means the rider must use soft "giving" hands, as the horse moving forward in a vigorous fox trot will exhibit plenty of head nodding. This nodding be facilitated by the rider, though trying to obtain or increase the head nod by "pumping" the reins will not result in improved action. The hands should be soft and following. Correct action is generated through plenty of forward impulsion created by the rider's seat and legs.

The even, people-oriented temperament of the MFT makes them ideal first mounts, or "baby-sitter" horses. Below (l to r), Jami and Brooke Walker take their fox trotters, Desporado and Angel, through their paces.

Photo courtesy of Terry Walker

Above, Rex Walker and his stallion Cody's Mustard Man take to Colorado's trails, where Cody demonstrates his ground-covering fox trot. Below, Rex asks Cody for less extension, and he naturally performs a gait that used to be termed the "fox walk," but which is actually a less extended, slower fox trot.

Apollo Traveller C, Registered Missouri Fox Trotting Horse

Photo by Terex Images

HEAVENLY GAITS

If a fox trotter tends to prefer a true trot or pace, the same corrective measures described in the Tennessee Walking Horse chapter should be used. Since the fox trot is bred into the horse, even moderately experienced riders will generally achieve good results on their own without having to resort to special training devices—provided they have plenty of motivation, patience and time to work things out. No horse can be trained, or retrained, on a hurried schedule.

PROMINENT SHOWS AND SALES

Besides the annual M.F.T.H.B.A. Show and Celebration held in Ava, Missouri each September, there is a Three Year old Futurity and Youth show held on the same grounds during the summer. Currently there are regional shows for the Missouri Fox Trotter over most of the United States. Up-to-date listings of these events are available through the MFTHBA office. The *Missouri Fox Trotting Journal*, an official MFT;HBA publication, also regularly publishes information about upcoming shows, trail rides, sales and other Missouri Fox Trotter related events.

FUTURE OF THE MISSOURI FOX TROTTER

At the time of this writing there are nearly 44,000 registered Missouri Fox Trotters. The burgeoning popularity of gaited horses in general, and of this horse in particular, is likely to increase this number substantially over the next few years. Regional fox trotter horse clubs have sprung up in every part of the U.S., as well as in Canada and Mexico. People who work with the fox trotter often become enthusiastic breed ambassadors.

While the Missouri Fox Trotting Horse Breed Association offers many important services to members and interested parties, they do not have a large and sophisticated advertising campaign, nor do they produce an expensive glossy magazine, to promote their horse. They don't require ambitious marketing, as these talented, athletic, beautiful, level-headed, smooth-gaited and versatile horses are invariably their own best advertisement.

—Chapter Five—
The Icelandic Horse

Icelanders liken the appearance of Americans on their tall, rangy horses to "birds in a tree." It is understandable that we should appear odd to them upon our massive equines, as Icelandic Horses seldom stand over 14 hands tall. But as any Icelander, or owner of Icelandic Horses, can attest, small stature in no way equates to small talent or abilities. Icelandic Horses have proved they can do everything their taller cousins can do—and in many cases, they can do it better.

The Icelandic Horse is the purest breed of horse in the world, having been isolated on an island and bred without outside influence for over one thousand years. He is valued for his easy, ground covering saddle gait—known as the *tolt*—as well as for other extraordinary qualities that has enabled this breed to survive, and thrive, under the most difficult and challenging of circumstances. This is a horse with a nature and physical constitution that is as tough as the land that shaped him.

LAND THAT SHAPED THE HORSE

Iceland is a basalt rock island in the North Atlantic ocean. It is a land known for sudden violent gales of hail, sleet, rain and snow, volcanic eruptions, quicksand mires, fierce and treacherous rivers, steaming hot water springs and geysers, boiling mud craters, quicksand bogs, wind storms, treeless vistas, vast deserts, as well as massive glaciers and rocky, mountain-

123

ous terrain. Its summers are too short for the ripening of grain, its fall and winters invariably dark, wet and bitterly cold.

On the other hand, Iceland's coastal weather is generally mild, being tempered as it is by the Gulf Stream. The limitless summer skies boast a midnight sun, while eerily beautiful northern lights illumine the polar winter. Iceland's rivers teem with salmon, its mountainside cliffs are nesting grounds for thousands of birds such as the exotic Puffin, its waterfalls, hot springs and geysers give birth to many-hued rainbows, and its native flowers—set amid sylvan glades and lush valley meadows—are so brilliantly colored that they appear to be illumined from within.

Iceland often casts a spell of enchantment upon unwary visitors with its rugged character and primitive, paradoxical beauty. The poet W.H. Auden visited Iceland in 1936, and returned there again in 1964. He later wrote:

"In my childhood dreams, Iceland was holy ground; when at the age of twenty-nine, I saw it for the first time, the reality verified my dream; at fifty-seven it was holy ground still, with the most magical light of anywhere on earth."

EARLY SETTLERS

Despite its allure, it can be fairly claimed that were it not for horses Iceland would never have become a settled country. The treacherous climate and landscape would have prevented even the hardy, bold Vikings from exploration and homesteading.

Northern Germanic Vikings sailed toward Iceland in a bid to escape the tyrannical rule of King Harald Fairhair of Norway, carrying household goods and livestock in the holds of their huge dragon ships. In 874 the first of these Nordic Vikings, Ingolfur Arnason, headed deliberately for the island that had previously only been described by Viking sailors who had been blown off course. Once in sight of this fabled land, Ingolfur followed an accepted Viking practice and took two carved wooden posts that normally flanked the Norwegian master's household chair—known as high seat pillars—and threw them overboard. He then pulled ashore on the southwest coast at the spot where these pillars drifted to shore, and there he and his shipmates settled. Since that location was steamy with hot springs Ingolfur named it "The Bay of Smoke" or, in Old Norse, Reykjavik.

ANCIENT NORDIC HORSEMANSHIP

Before settling Iceland Nordic peoples had a long history of horsemanship as well as seamanship. They called their ships "horses of the sea," and on-land entertainment—which in keeping with their tempestuous natures were commonly grudge-solving duels—consisted of horse races or stallion fights. Roman historian Tacitus, in 98 A.D., wrote about the Germanic people in his book *Germania*. In this work he states that these people possessed excellent horses, which were the pastime of children, the aim of young men and much indulged in by old men. In chapter ten of the above named work he states:

"But what is unique about this nation is that it tries to obtain omens and predictions from horses. The animals are reared at

public expense in the afore-mentioned sacred woods. The horses are snow-white and have never been used for any non-sacred work, and when they have been harnessed to the divine chariot they are accompanied by the priest, the king, or the head of state, who studies their neighs or snorts. No oracle is more sacred than these horses, not only among the populace but also among the chief-tains, for although the Germans regard the priests as the servants of the Lord they regard the horses as his confidants."

Nearly eight centuries later, Nordic settlers of the barren island of Iceland continued to rely heavily upon the horse—who was honored with the title *parfasti pjonninn*, or "most useful servant", a well-deserved honor. Iceland's rugged, unpredictable terrain didn't allow for wheeled vehicles of any kind. Therefore, the Icelandic Horse was used for carrying people, lumber, household goods—even coffins—cross-country on its sturdy little back.

Icelanders also continued to bestow mystical powers upon its head. Some settlers, upon sailing into shore, immediately set a horse loose on land. Wherever that horse stopped to graze, the people would settle.

OF HORSES AND SAGAS

The *Sagas of Icelanders* is among the world's oldest extant body of literature, and written in Old Norse. The Icelandic language has changed so little over the centuries that even Icelandic children can still read and understand the Sagas. This would be comparable to English speaking youngsters reading and understanding Shakespeare. Because of the impor-tance of horses to the early culture of Iceland, there are a great number of Sagas that cast horses in main roles. One such saga, which typifies many, translates as follows:

"At that time a ship came to Kolbeinsaros laden with livestock, but they lost a mare into Brimnes Forest which Thorir Pigeon-nose bought, if it should ever be found. Later he did find it. It was the

swiftest of horses and called Fluga (Fly). A man named Orn (Eagle) was a vagabond and skilled in black magic. He lay in wait for Thorir in Hvinverjadal when he was going south across Kjol and made a bet with Thorir as to whose horse would be first, because he had quite a good horse. Each man put up a hundred in silver. They both rode south across Kjol until they came to a plain, which now is called Pigeon-nose's Course. The difference in speed was so great that Thorir met Orn in the middle of the course.

Orn was so dissatisfied with his financial loss that he did not want to live and went up to the mountain, which is now called Arnarfell (Eagle's Mount), and there took his own life, but Fluga was so much out of breath that she was left there. When Thorir came back from the Althing (government assembly) he found a white horse with a gray mane with Fluga, and with him she had conceived a foal. She gave birth to Eidfaxi, who was taken abroad and who killed seven people in one day at Mjors (in Norway) and then was killed himself. Fluga was lost in a bog at Flugumyri (Fly's Swamp)."

The early settlers of this northern island tended to be highly mystical and superstitious. They credited mountains, woods and rivers with particular spirits, and their lore is rich with allusion to the unseen world. Even today many Icelanders believe in ghosts, trolls, elves and other assorted malignant and benign spirits.

Just as horses were central to the Icelandic culture, so were they central to many of the mystical beliefs of the people, including one Icelandic custom of cursing enemies. Icelanders erected "scorn poles" to cause their enemies' downfall or humiliation. The great poet-Viking Egil Skallagrimsson erected such a scorn pole against Queen Gunnhild and King Eirik Bloodaxe, which was credited with driving the pair from their kingdom. That saga explains the scorn pole curse:

"He (Egil) took a hazel pole in his hand and went to a certain jutting rock facing the mainland. Then he took a horse's head and

set it up on the pole. Afterwards he recited a formula, saying these words: 'I here set up a scorn against King Eirik and Queen Gunnhild.' He turned the horse's head landwards. 'I turn this scorn upon the landspirits which dwell in this land, so that they all fare wildering ways, and none light on or lie in his dwelling till they drive King Eirik and Gunnhild out of the land.' Next he jammed the pole down into a crack in the rock and let it stand there. The head he turned landwards, but he graved runes on the pole and they state all that formula."

The King and Queen were subsequently forced to flee Norway which, according to the Saga, was directly attributable to Egil's scorn pole curse.

GOVERNMENT OF ICELAND

Though the geography and climate of Iceland may be elementary, its people are far from uncivilized. This country boasts the oldest democratic government in the world. Within a half-century from the time Vikings laid claim to the island it became evident that, if left unchecked, Iceland was in danger of becoming a nest of violent, pillaging and murderous thieves; worse, men with might, rather than wisdom, would gain the power to rule. To avoid this fate, a wise man named Ulfljot traveled to Norway to study that nation's legal code, and make recommendations for a body of law for Iceland. Ulfljot's brother, Grim, stayed behind and chose a permanent spot for the seat of Iceland's new government.

In 930 the first government assembly (Althing) met in a spot later named Thingvellir. Thingvellir is located in a wide valley north of Thingvallavatn, Iceland's largest lake. Grim's choice of locations was perfect, as the valley is overshadowed by a 150-foot cliff over which the Oxara River plunges in a magnificent waterfall before winding along the foot of the precipice and joining the Thingvallavatn Lake. Opposite the cliff is a view that encompasses ice-capped mountains. Beautiful, temperate Thingvellir has become the most revered location in Iceland.

Not only did the Althing from the first oversee a body of democratic laws, but it served a vital social function as well. Icelanders were, and are, a gregarious gossipy people who would undertake the dangerous journey to Althing upon their hardy horses with hardly a second thought. Once there, grievances and disputes were brought before the national assembly, where they were adjudicated. An equally important purpose of the Althing was the opportunity it allowed Icelanders for gossip and socializing. The annual event became a national celebration, and was always attended by a great many Icelanders. This is still true today. When the Althing celebrated its 1,100 anniversary in 1974, 50,000 people—almost one quarter of the country's population—attended.

Then, as now, travel across the country meant braving violent, unpredictable storms, fording treacherous rivers, and crossing bogs that likely as not had bottoms of quicksand. The mounts these people used for such journeys had to be extraordinarily sensible, intuitive, sure-footed, brave, strong swimmers, and possess an acutely accurate sense of direction. The small, smooth-gaited muscular horses that had been imported in large numbers from Western Norway and the British Isles possessed these qualities. Selective breeding, combined with the law of survival of the fittest further enhanced them.

HORSES A NATIONAL TREASURE

Iceland has no natural predators to prey upon the horse population, which undoubtedly contributed to the small equine's apparent lack of fear—to this day they almost never spook under saddle. But their isolation from other horse populations made them vulnerable to outside diseases. To guard against such diseases decimating their valued horse herds, one of the first official acts of the Althing of 930 was to declare illegal the further importation of horses to Iceland. This ban on imported horses remains until the present day. Though horses may be exported to other countries, once they leave the shores of Iceland, they can never return. Thus, in effect, there have been "closed books" on the Icelandic breed for over one thousand years.

This explains why the Icelandic Horse invariably possesses the pure, smooth lateral saddle gaits, since up until the late 1600's trotting horses in

HEAVENLY GAITS

Europe were the exception, rather than the rule. Later on, once trotters caught on in other nations, Iceland was never tempted to import them, as carriage travel was nearly impossible over the island's rugged terrain. Their small, smooth gaited, easily-kept, rugged and sensible saddle horses continued to suit the Icelanders' needs.

ICELAND'S HORSE MANAGEMENT

The Icelandic Horse has traditionally been raised in a near-wild state on large tracts of land bordering the coast of Iceland—the interior of Iceland is unpopulated and considered inhabitable. All the horses are gathered "into the fold" in Mid-September for the massive sheep roundup that takes place every year. Farmers from each district cooperate to gather their sheep (which are also a unique, pure old strain) from the common grazing land in the interior. Even today, the horse is essential to this work, as wheeled vehicles cannot traverse the interior of the island. (In fact, Iceland still has only one major road—Ring Road—so-named because it forms a ring around the edge of the island.) Sheep roundup may last for a week, during which time the farmers sleep in mountainside huts or natural caves. The horses rest at night

Turned out to forage for the winter, these horses grow long, shaggy coats and independent natures.

Photo courtesy of Ann Ellwell

In Iceland, most mares foal unassisted with few difficulties. Foals are raised with little human intervention until they are old enough for early training.

in stone pens that dot the interior. These same pens and huts or grottos may be used during the summer months for overnight stays of "pony trekkers." Pony trekking—days-long trail rides through the interior—has become a popular pastime for Iceland's tourist trade.

Following the extremely difficult work of roundup, a carefully selected band of 15-25 brood mares is turned back out for the winter with a chosen stud, and the herd fends for itself over the long winter and spring months. As might be expected, these animals become rugged and independent over the season as they grow long, shaggy winter hair coats and paw through ice and snow for forage—though some farmers set out barrels of herring as supplement, which the horses eat sparingly. This treatment has produced horses who maintain their condition on 20% less feed than other equines of equal size.

There is a 95% rate of fertility for these naturally bred horses (as compared to under 50% for hand-bred horses). In the spring mares foal unassisted, and there are few problems. This may attributed to the horses' tough constitution, but also undoubtedly to the fact that over many centuries those mares and foals who died during the birthing process were unable to pass on their genetically heritable weaknesses to the next generation. So by the process of natural elimination only horses with the genetic potential for hardiness, fertility and good breeding conformation have survived.

This process of natural selection was enhanced by the pragmatic practices of early Icelanders. Though they had high regard for their horses—and even insisted that they possess a strongly sociable character—they never lapsed into sentimentality. Horses that were in any way inferior were simply butchered and eaten. Also, early in Iceland's history the cruel practice of stallion fights was common, and horse racing was a national passion. So the horses allowed—and able—to survive and multiply in Iceland were extraordinarily strong and fast. They were sensible, self-sufficient and independent, feisty yet sociable. They were sure-footed on land, and able to ford sometimes wild, unpredictable bodies of water. They possessed speed and were comfortable to ride. These are still typical qualities of the modern Icelandic Horse.

After foaling season horses are once more gathered up and herded together into huge "sorting pens." Here they are separated and sorted, their rightful ownership being determined by an earmark that is registered with the government. Foals are earmarked before being set free in summer pastures with other youngstock. Older horses are kept for training and/or use over the summer, after which they will be set free to rest until the fall sheep roundup. The late spring gathering is a festive occasion when Icelanders enjoy a lively round of "one-upmanship" in the form of horse trading. Icelanders pride themselves on their keen horse trading skills. The one drawback to this is that, once a horse is traded, there's no guarantee he'll stay with his new owner! Icelandic Horses possess an extraordinarily acute "homing instinct," and are prone to running back to their previous homes and pastures, even from great distances.

The "up" side to this latter trait is that Icelandic Horses have an uncanny sense of direction, and can be trusted to bring their riders safely home even over long distances.

STATE CONTROLLED BREEDING

Today, Icelandic Horse breeding is coordinated by the state, which has divided Iceland into four breeding districts. About half the horses are still raised in the traditional manner—except that the fields that bands of horses are run on are now enclosed. Strict records on the production and disposal of these horses are maintained by The Agricultural Society of Iceland. Restrictions have been placed on loose grazing, particularly of stallions, so many farms now breed and raise their horses in stables. Some traditionalists worry that this might eventually result in some decline in the robustness of the breed—though this is unlikely considering the rigorous evaluations stallions and brood mares are subject to.

Horses are strictly evaluated for their breeding and performance potential, and horse judging approaches the status of religion among Icelandic Horse owners. The most important criterion for the Icelandic Horse is that it possess good gaits—the comfortable 4-beat tolt being of prime consideration. Horses must also meet strict conformational standards. They must prove highly trainable, and a willing mount. Horses displaying any inclination toward a poor disposition are immediately disqualified as breeding stock.

STRICT BREEDING STANDARDS

Horses that have been used extensively for breeding are evaluated on the quality of their offspring. Stallions whose offspring meet an exceptionally high and consistent standard of excellence—as judged by government representatives at regional shows—are honored with the title "Honor Prize Stallion." So far only four stallions have ever been awarded this honor: Sorli 653 from Sautharkroki; Thattur 722 from Kirkjubae; Hrafn 802 from Holtsmula; and Ofeigur 882, from Flugumyri. (The numbers following their names are state pedigree numbers, followed by the name of the farm from which the horse originated.)

HEAVENLY GAITS

FAMILY LINE TRAITS

When considering the purchase of a horse from one of these lines, it helps to know that each of the families of above horses possess certain characteristics peculiar to their breeding. Sorli 653 (pronounced Sortley) horses are known for demonstrating tremendous energy. They are easily "formed," or influenced by their trainer. This characteristic is prized enough to make them highly valuable, though Sorli horses may possess coarse heads.

Thattur 722 breeding produces a chestnut colored horse with refined, light bones, well-defined heads and necks, and very cooperative dispositions.

Hrafn 802 (pronounced Raff), breeding produces exceptionally beautiful heads, as well as elegant, long necks and refined conformation. These horses are sweet-natured and very willing under saddle. This breeding, however, is considered less predictable than other top lines, since Hrafn horses have not been line-bred for as long as some other families of horses. Nevertheless, it is generally agreed that Hrafn blood guarantees quality.

Breeding from Ofeigur 882 stock produces a horse with great presence, power and boldness. These horses are independent thinkers, and generally require experienced, tactful riders.

GOVERNMENT REGULATED HORSE MANAGEMENT

Southern Iceland is much more climatically and geographically inhospitable than the northern coast. Northern Iceland's coastal farms are particularly well-known for its horse breeding operations, and this includes the district of Skagafjordur. In 1879 authorities from that district appointed a three-man committee in each parish to oversee the improvement of horse breeding practices in the district, which practice was soon adopted in other regions. The governmental bodies of Iceland have, since the first Althing, always been closely involved with the regulation and breeding of Icelandic Horses. This would be considered restrictive and unacceptable in the United States, but is mostly viewed as reasonable by the sensible Icelander, since horses are one of the country's most valuable natural resources.

When horses began to be exported from Iceland to European nations in large numbers in the 1970's, the Icelandic Farmers Association expressed concern about the possibility of losing some of their best breeding stock to foreign interests. The government responded by levying a 10% tax on all horses sold for export. Now if an especially valued brood mare or stallion is being considered by a buyer for export, monies raised from this tax can be used by the government to purchase the horse. This ensures that the "best of the best" remains in Iceland, while the breeder isn't financially penalized for producing a good horse.

Another concern of the Farmers Association was that Icelandic Horses continue to be bred for consistently high quality. They feared that people with less history and depth of knowledge concerning the breed might not be able to maintain the standards adhered to in Iceland. In September of 1974 a committee of interested parties met to formulate a set of common breeding standards and a judging system for the Icelandic Horse. These standards were adopted by the International Federation of Icelandic Horses (FEIF) These standards are now strictly adhered to worldwide, making Icelandic Horses the only breed to be judged by identical criteria in every nation.

THE STORY OF FEIF

In the late 1950's through to the latter part of the 1960's the Icelandic Horse was quickly gaining popularity all over Europe. The Icelandic state breeding secretary, Gunnar Bjarnason, was largely responsible for introducing and promoting his nation's horse to Europeans. On May 24, 1969, at the annual German tolt championships held in Whitsun, Germany, a small group of people representing independent Icelandic Horse associations from Germany, Switzerland, Austria, Denmark and Holland, in cooperation with Iceland, formed the Federation of Friends of the Icelandic Horse (now named the International Federation of Iceland Horse Owners but still commonly shortened to FEIF). At that meeting the first temporary board was elected, and included Gunnar Bjarnanson, Walter Feldmannsen., Ewald Isenbugel, Max Indermaru, and Gunnar Jonsson. This group was responsible for formulating the Federation's first statutes. It was decided at this first meeting that a European Championship for Icelandic Horses would be held the following year, in Germany.

Currently a World Iceland Horse Championship is held every other year, with the location of, and responsibility for, the event rotating among the various FEIF-Associated countries. FEIF now includes ten European nations, Canada and the United States.

CONFORMATION STANDARDS

The Icelandic Horse stands between 12.2 and 14.2 hands, with a well conformed, muscular build. Though his size qualifies him to be classified as a "pony," Icelanders give their horse the honor due him by calling him "hest," or horse—there is no Icelandic word for pony. Despite his size, the Icelandic Horse has the ability to carry a proportionally greater amount of weight than his larger equine cousins. This is attributed to a hardy constitution, short, solid coupling, and extremely dense bone structure.

Icelandic Horses are late maturing, and seldom begin training under saddle until their fifth year. They are very long-lived, however—horses in their twenties are often still ridden, and mares may continue to be used successfully as brood mares until their mid-twenties.

This horse generally has a fine, well-sculpted head with expressive eyes. The skin (in summer) should be thin with a fine coat of hair. The judging standards point out that this serves more than an aesthetic purpose, as many people believe that horses with thin skin and well-defined bones are more sensitive and attentive mounts than are coarse, thick-skinned horses. The jaw-bone should be large, the teeth well-formed and set into the jaw in an appropriate manner. Ears should be small, narrow and pointed at the tips, and demonstrate a lively, friendly temperament. Manes are abundant, and may fall on both sides of the neck.

The neck should be approximately as long as the horse's head, well set into a long, sloping shoulder, and carried high. Withers are long and prominent; the back should be medium length, strong and exceptionally supple. The back is tightly coupled to the croup, with smooth loins that are neither peaked nor ridged. The croup itself must be long, sloping and muscular. For a horse to demonstrate a top quality tolt, there should be a 95-

The Icelandic Horse should have a fine, well-sculpted head. Left, Elding fra Refstaad exhibits the character that Icelandic Horse lovers look for.

Photo courtesy of Helms Hill Farms

100 degree angle between the pelvis and thigh. Loin muscling should carry well down the thigh. The tail should be set on low and carried with freedom of movement and expression.

Limbs usually exhibit extraordinary substance, with clean bone and correct angles. In front the forearm should be longer than the cannon; in back the thigh and gaskin are longer than the cannon. Pasterns should be moderately long and sloping. Joints should be large and well-defined, with clean connections to the bone. The horse should move with straight, springy steps and no hint of interference.

The Icelandic Horse's feet should be well shaped, have good quality horn, a large supple frog, and be an appropriate size for the individual.

HORSE OF A DIFFERENT COLOR

A few large farms in Iceland are known for raising their horses for a particular color. Kirkjubaer in South Iceland is probably the largest and most well known of these, and specializes in producing red horses with light manes and tails. Overall this is the exception to the rule, however, and Icelanders pride themselves on the wide spectrum of Icelandic Horse colors. Horse breeders sometimes claim that the only time color is discussed among horsemen is when other more important attributes are lacking. Icelandic Horses can be found in fifteen official basic types of colors and color

137

combinations, with each of these types subdivided into several other more precise categories. Red, bay and black horses are most common, followed by gray, dun, palomino, albino-bay and albino. Often Icelandic Horses sport gray or silver manes and tails, and mouse-gray horses with silver manes and tails are especially striking to the eye.

Characteristics of prime importance in the international breeding standards were described as follows in the booklet *Judging Icelandic Breeding Horses*, published by FEIF:

> *The Icelandic Horse must be a true riding horse, courageous, cheerful, trustworthy, spirited and cooperative. It must command at least four gaits, of which one must be tolt, and should preferably also have flying pace. It must be strong, enduring and have a long useful life. It must be frugal, robust and inexpensive to keep.*

As may be surmised from the above, a great deal of importance is attached to the temperament of the Icelandic Horse. Even if an animal is near-perfect in every other regard, any demonstration for meanness or unwillingness under saddle can be grounds to disqualify it as a breeding animal. But more than this, Icelanders expect their horses to be downright sociable and personable, with unique qualities of character and temperament. These qualities are supposed to be evident in the horse's expression, carriage and demeanor. Such a horse is highly regarded in his native land.

GAITS OF THE ICELANDIC HORSE

The Icelandic Horse may possess either four or five gaits under saddle: Walk, trot, tolt, gallop and/or flying pace. The gaits are of such importance in judging these horses that people desiring to become recognized judges for the breed must be riders or ex-riders.

The flat walk should be performed with long, fluid movements and good rhythm, with the print of the hind foot disfiguring the print of the forefoot.

Icelandic Horsemen who use the horses for cross country work do not post the trot, and prefer horses with a flat, comfortable trot with little suspension or action—a "farmer's trot." The more "continental" type of Icelandic trot, however, demonstrates a kind of "floating" action, with smooth suspension and long strides. In gaited and dressage competitions this type of trot, combined with more animation, generally gives the horse an advantage over the more common type of trot. If a horse is to be used for traveling cross-country, however, the farmers trot is the most practical and comfortable version of this gait.

Though horses are judged and scored on all five gaits (which may put 4-gaited horses at a slight disadvantage in international competition), the tolt is by far the most important gait of the Icelandic Horse. Essentially, it is the same ground-covering, even 4-beat gait as the running walk, or paso llano. When performed at speed it becomes a flashy, animated show rack.

The tolt is performed with a high, proud head carriage, good overstride, and smooth rhythm. The horse should demonstrate the ability to collect and extend at the tolt, and be able to perform the gait over varying terrain.

The Icelandic Horse pace is known as *skied*, or the "flying pace," this latter for good reason. As with any pacing horse, a slow pace is considered highly undesirable. In fact, photos of horses performing this gait demonstrate that the "flying pace" is actually a stepping pace—or broken, 4-beat pace---performed at extraordinary speed. Horses who perform the flying pace can travel short distances up to 30 miles per hour, and really do seem to be airborne at times. Pace races are one of the most exciting of Icelandic Horse competitions. Though the ideal flying pace exhibits substantial "float" during suspension, the lateral side-to-side action of this gait combined with its speed requires an extremely talented and experienced rider.

Icelandic Horses races are performed at the 4-beat gallop. Otherwise there is little use for the gait in that country. The 3-beat canter is considered unsightly altogether. But in international competition judges look for an even three-beat canter performed with loose action and boldness, combined with control. Five-gaited horses often have trouble maintaining a three-beat canter, and judges may make allowances for this. Whether the gait is 3-beat or 4-beat, cross cantering is always reason for low judging marks.

Above, Blaeugur demonstrated a fast tolt in perfect form at FEIF's 1991 World Championships in Norrkoping, Sweden. Sara Conklin up. Below, two riders in flying pace at Devon Horse Show Exhibition, 1988.

Photo courtesy of Helms Hill Farms

Photo courtesy of Helms Hill Farms

ICELANDIC HORSE TACK

Saddles are of the European or English style, often with padded seats, break-away irons, and cruppers. Bridles are also European in design, made of leather, with browbands and cavessons. Snaffle bits are common, as are loose-jointed Icelandic bits with long shanks attached to rings at either side of the mouthpiece. Given the speed and extreme forward action of the flying pace horses, these latter bits can sometimes be a necessity if the rider is to maintain control over the horse!

Since willingness is an important criterion for the Icelandic Horse, whips are seldom necessary. In fact, riders of Icelandic Horses are more like to have to cope with too much willingness rather than not enough. A judge will fault a horse's willingness if he notes that the rider must use a whip to generate good forward motion.

Wedges, pads, weighted shoes and other artificial training devices are strictly prohibited in competitive events among Icelandic Horses.

SHOWING AND USING THE ICELANDIC HORSE

Though autos, jeeps and buses have taken the place of horses for everyday transportation in Iceland, the islanders still use their horses for everyday pleasure riding, pony trekking, sheep herding, and competitive events. Large numbers of riders are invariably traversing the countryside around the suburbs of cities like Reykjavik during weekends and evenings. Pony treks may be large or small in number, and as easy or difficult as the desire and capabilities of those who participate. Some groups take a leisurely one-or-two day shallow excursions into areas surrounding the coast. Other trekking groups ride for many days or weeks in the interior.

Pony treks take riders through desolate valleys, deserts and lava fields, across turbulent uncertain rivers, and through bogs and swamps. They may swim with their horses in natural pools formed by hot springs. Riders sleep in caves or huts, while the horses grab what little forage they can in antique, stone-fenced pastures. Such rides are a challenge for any horseman—but would not be popular were they not as exhilarating as they are exhausting.

Photo by Phil Pretty, courtesy of Christine Swartz

Above, Borkur, a gelding who is 20+ years of age, is ready to take Joan Pretty for a Sunday drive. Borkur is owned by Robyn Hood.

HORSE CLUBS AND ORGANIZATIONS

Iceland has a remarkable tradition of organized horse meetings. There are more than forty riding clubs on the island, which membership forms the basis for The National Association of Riding Clubs. This body of horsemen organizes country-wide horse meets every four years, in various districts. At these meets horses are shown, raced, paraded, judged, bought and sold with great enthusiasm. Thousands of horsemen make the journey to these meets on horseback, often while driving dozens of other horses along, or while leading a string of two to eight other horses. Ponying a string of horses along is a unique Icelandic talent that is much taken for granted in that country—but horsemen may be judged for their skill at this in competition in other nations. It is awe-inspiring to see thousands of Icelandic Horses all gathered together in one place, where they resemble a massive canvas of power, animation and color.

The riding clubs from each district organize large horse meets on a rotational basis during those years when there is no country-wide meet. The country-wide meet and the district meets offer members of the Agricultural

Society of Iceland an opportunity for judging horses for breeding potential, and for getting horses officially registered. Also, the various clubs organize their own gallop races, with a committee appointed by the NARC setting the dates.

European competition under the FEIF banner includes judging events for tolt, four-gaited horses, five-gaited horses, pace, cross country events, and dressage. Five-gaited races require that a horse race at the gallop, then switch to flying pace at precisely 50 meters. International competition has also included steeplechasing and drilling.

PROVEN ENDURANCE

The Icelandic Horse's extraordinary stamina and endurance was handily demonstrated in North American during two endurance races held during the U.S. Bicentennial in 1976. The first of these was The Great American Horse Race, which started on May 31 in Frankfort, New York and ended on September 5, nearly 3,000 miles away, in Sacramento, California. Fifty-two riders from Australia, France, Germany, Canada, Switzerland, Austria, Iceland and the U.S. participated in this race, which was the longest one ever organized. Two riders with four Icelandic Horses entered the race, and both these riders finished, one in 13th place. The second of these two riders tragically lost a horse to poisoned drinking water. He rode the last 625 miles on a single Icelandic Horse, which resulted in his dropping from 7th to 21st place.

That same summer eight Icelandic Horses with four riders participated in The Pony Express Race, which covered the nearly 2,000 miles between St. Joseph, Missouri and Sacramento, California. In addition to these there were ten other riders mounted on Arabian and Appaloosa horses. All four of the Icelandic Horse riders reached their destination, while only four of the ten other riders (fewer than half) were able to complete the race. Not only did these small horses demonstrate they could "go the distance," but they proved even hardier than the Arabian horses, who are world renowned for strength and endurance. At the daily vet checks along these race courses the Icelandic Horses were noted for their excellent condition and continued willing attitudes.

HEAVENLY GAITS

A FAMILY MOUNT

Though the Icelandic Horse is outstanding in nearly any type of equestrian competitive event, his most useful purpose is perhaps that of family pleasure horse. Few horses are more sheer *fun* to ride. Since the Icelandic seldom spooks, he is extremely easy to ride and handle. He also tends to be sure-footed, sensible and small in size. Even young children can mount and ride him safely. His strength, endurance, willingness and versatility make him a perfect mount for adults. Even large people can ride this diminutive horse, since he has perhaps the greatest weight-carrying ability per pound than any other horse. His proud carriage and great heart more than makes up for his small size. The Icelandic's smaller size can actually be a great morale booster for people who are intimidated by larger horses.

The Icelandic Horse is known to possess an uncannily accurate "homing instinct," which can be an invaluable aid on the trail. This isn't surprising, considering the breed's history. Few other types of horses are as social, sweet-natured and trustworthy as the Icelandic Horse—who still is a "most useful servant" under saddle.

And speaking of "under saddle," let's not forget that remarkably smooth tolt. . .

Photo courtesy of Ragnarok Farms

—Chapter Six—
The Peruvian Paso

The Peruvian Paso is a unique animal with a long and extraordinary history. Though relatively few in number (fewer than 50,000 worldwide), this breed deserves a prominent place as one of the world's finest breeds of gaited horse.

It has been claimed that Peruvians—particularly Peruvian Horse breeders—are among the most patient people on earth. This must be so, since their horses have been purebred for nearly 400 years, yet modern breeders of Peruvian Paso horses still strive for improvement. They are willing to go to almost any lengths to create a horse that lives up to their image of equine perfection, no matter how long it may take, nor how many less-than-acceptable animals must be culled from their breeding programs.

UNIQUE CHARACTERISTICS

This kind of idealistic dedication has enabled Peruvian breeders to produce a docile, easy to train horse which exhibits proud carriage and a fiery presence. Horses that display this paradoxical combination of qualities are said to have *brio*. Another unique feature of this horse is its natural smooth four-beat riding gait, called the *paso llano*. The paso llano, a type of stepping pace, is inherited by every purebred Peruvian Horse. The Peruvian Paso also performs a fast broken pace, which is called the *sobreando*. Horses travelling

HEAVENLY GAITS

in this gait reach speeds averaging 15 miles per hour or more.

All Peruvian bred riding horses also exhibit *termino*. Termino describes the distinctive action displayed by the front quarters of the Peruvian Paso when he performs his gait. It is this action that sets the Peruvian Horse's gait apart from every other horse in the world.

TRUE TERMINO

Termino is a graceful movement where the forelegs are smoothly rolled dramatically toward the outside, loosely from the shoulder, with an outward flexion of the knee and fetlock joints, with each step the horse takes—rather like a swimming motion. The legs of a fast, smooth moving horse with great termino has been described as resembling flashing eggbeaters when viewed from the front.

To the uninitiated this action may appear to be a fault, rather like severe winging or paddling, which in a non-Peruvian Horse would usually be a compensation for crooked front limbs. But termino is not caused by anything incorrect or weak in the Peruvian Paso's conformation.

Horses that paddle tend to land their weight first on the inside edge of their hoof, wearing away that edge of the foot and causing (or exacerbating) a toed-in conformation. Horses that wing usually first strike the ground with the outside edge of their front foot, thus wearing the hoof wall away unevenly to the outside, and causing (or increasing) a toed-out conformation.

The Peruvian Horse's front foot lands squarely on the ground, regardless of the amount of termino he exhibits. The action of termino originates in the shoulder, and is exhibited even by horses with beautifully conformed forequarters.

It was once widely surmised that termino evolved as an easier means for the Peruvian Horse to cope with his long treks through loose desert sands. Whether or not this historical assumption is true, termino has become a highly valued characteristic of the Peruvian breed.

Photo by Barbara J. Wright, courtesy of Rancho de Colores

This photo of *H.N. Iqueno demonstrates the Peruvian Paso characteristics of brio and termino. This bold stallion is gaiting perfectly at liberty—note how the front foot "rolls out" from the shoulder.

HEAVENLY GAITS

PERUVIAN PASO *NOT* A PASO FINO

People not closely associated with the Peruvian Paso sometimes fail to differentiate between this breed and the Paso Fino. To many people's way of thinking, a *paso* horse is a *paso* horse. (Paso means *step* in Spanish.) In an effort to distinguish their horse from the Paso Fino, breeders and promoters of the Peruvian Paso often elect to call their animal the Peruvian Horse. This desire to separate the two breeds is understandable, since aside from the fact that both types of horses boast lateral riding gaits—though not identical gaits—the Peruvian Paso is an entirely distinct breed from the Paso Fino.

VERY EARLY HISTORY

The Peruvian Horse has been purely bred from Spanish stock for almost 500 years, with little or no outside influences. The first Spanish horses landed in horseless South America with Captain Francisco Pizarro and his conquistadors in 1530. These men conquered Peru for the Spanish crown upon the backs of sturdy, durable war horses, mostly of Spanish Andaluse/Barb breeding. These horses did not themselves make the harrowing sea journey from Spain to Peru. The majority traveled to Peru from Panama and the Spanish horse breeding centers that were by then well established on Santo Domingo and the other Caribbean Islands.

But these first horses to land in South America weren't the forebears to the Peruvian Paso Horse. The horses Spaniards used for packing and for war were walk, trot and canter horses. It is highly improbable that such strong trotting stock had anything whatever to do with the creation of a strongly gaited ambling horse, such as the Peruvian Paso.

Soon after the Spanish settled in Peru, the mid-coastal city of Lima was the cultural and commercial capitol of South America, and within a short while it became the most important city in the hemisphere. During the Spanish colonial period the wealthiest, best educated and most influential people of Europe journeyed to Lima to settle in what was to become known as "The City of Kings."

During this time the Spanish were the foremost horse breeders of the world. It was only natural for those rich and influential people traveling to Peru to bring the best palfrys with them, and to import more fine horses once they settled. Only the very finest and hardiest horses were considered worthy, and able, to journey by sea all the way from Spain to Peru. These horses were the forebears to today's Peruvian Paso. Most of these imported riding horses were descended from Barb, Spanish Jennet, Andalusian and Friesian stock.

These horses were particularly fine in every respect, inheriting the best qualities of each of the aforementioned breeds. Both the Andalusian and the Friesian were valued for high, animated action, proud carriage, a cooperative but fiery spirit, and abundant mane and tail. In addition, the Andalusian was outstandingly beautiful, and the Friesian was a larger-than-average horse for its day. The latter blood helped contribute size to some of the Peruvian blood strains. The Barb boasted a lovely, well-balanced conformation, as well as the smooth lateral riding gaits that were so prized in early saddle horses. The Spanish Jennet was also an ambling horse and, though rather plain looking, was reputed to be the smoothest riding horse in the world.

With such useful and noble ancestry, the Peruvian Paso was destined to become a very special breed of horse.

DEVELOPMENT OF THE EARLY PERUVIAN PASO

By the mid-1600's Spain's stock of good saddle blood was becoming depleted at a time when she was embroiled in a number of wars and disputes, and needed all the horsepower she could muster. Mother Spain could no longer afford to send horses to Peru. The country's geographic isolation—it is bounded on all sides by jungles, oceans and mountain range—further prohibited the importation of horses. So Peruvian Horse breeders began to breed riding horses from the excellent gaited stock already on hand. Since they couldn't easily look to the rest of the world for standards and examples, these men set their own standards. They sought very unique qualities—such as brio, termino and the paso llano—in their horses. Because they couldn't import outside bloodlines, line breeding was practiced. By crossing closely related individuals they created horses which were highly prepotent, or likely to consistently produce horses true to type.

HEAVENLY GAITS

During this period the Peruvian Horse was one of the few to escape the influx of trotting blood that so heavily influenced the rest of the world's horses. Also, though carriage travel was the normal mode of travel in most of the civilized world, the rough mountainous terrain and heavy sands of Peru were not conducive to the building of roads for carriages. For many years after the world-wide decline in popularity of gaited riding horses, Peruvians continued to breed their *Cabalol Peruano de Paso*, or [smooth] walking Peruvian Horse.

Peruvian horsemen were so diligent in their efforts that by the latter part of the 16th century, just seventy years after Spain conquered Peru, horses of that previously horseless country were comparable to the world's finest. Around that time Inca historian de la Vega Garcilazo wrote: "From the horses that have multiplied in Peru, we find races as good as the best of Spain, among which we encounter some fit for the games as well as some good for the parades, work and travel." The Peruvian Paso horse as a distinct type was first acknowledged in a book by Felipe Gonzales de Vidaurre, published in 1780. A substantial body of written and artistic evidence demonstrates that by the nineteen hundreds, the Peruvian Paso was a prominent part of Peruvian culture.

INFLUENCES AFFECTING THE BREED

The modern Peruvian Paso is very much a product of the climatic, geographic and political influences of the country from which it springs. A basic knowledge about the country of Peru helps us understand the influences that significantly affected the development of the Peruvian Horse.

Peru consists of a wide strip of land laying along the (western) Pacific coast of South America. It is the continent's third largest country (see map). All along the Peruvian coast is an arid desert. To the east of this area is the Andes Mountains, which range runs along the middle—or "backbone"—portion of the country. The eastern, or Amazonian, side of this mountain range consists of densely jungled, semi-tropical lowlands that make for an even more formidable habitat than Peru's mountains and deserts.

The majority of Peru's population is located along the foothills of the Andes Mountains and in the arid coastal regions. This thin strip of land (150 -

250 miles wide) is geographically divided into the northern and southern coastal regions. Southern Peru is bounded by Chile and Bolivia, the northern portion by Ecuador. The central, coastal city of Lima is the dividing point between northern and southern Peru.

NORTHERN PERU

Peru's northern coastal region boasts large fertile valleys. Rivers that flow generally east to west from the Andes to the Pacific Ocean supply these valleys with sufficient water for large scale agriculture. For example, the Chicama River provides an agricultural oasis in the Chicama Valley, a region north of the coastal city of Trujillo. Northern Peruvian farmers grow a number of crops, including corn, rice, cotton and sugar; since the nineteenth century sugar has been by far the most important of these. Northern Peru is known for immense sugar plantations such as the Chicama Valley's Casa Grande, founded by the German immigrant Juan Gildermeister.

Northern Peru's capacity for producing sugar cane was enhanced by the agricultural and business acumen of families such as the Gildermeisters. Such settlers instituted complex modern irrigation and farming techniques that enabled the land to support ever larger sugar plantations.

The wealthy (and wily) Juan Gildermeister first settled in Peru in the mid 1800's. In the 1870's natural disasters and political upheaval caused by Peru's conflict with Chile forced most of the smaller, Peruvian-owned Haciendas in northern Peru into bankruptcy. The enterprising Gildermeister was one of the few landowners wealthy enough to withstand these influences; Gildermeister bought out many of the neighboring plantations. By 1925 the Casa Grande had grown, by means of such takeovers and by increasing productive land, to be the largest privately owned sugar plantation in the world. At that time Casa Grande consisted of an area roughly one-quarter the size of Switzerland.

Landowners on the great northern sugar plantations required horses with great strength and endurance. Hacienda owners and overseers used them for general travel and to survey their vast plantations---they rode them from hacienda to hacienda and from field to field. The horses these northern landowners used and bred usually carried Friesian blood, and were the nation's workhorse.

In keeping with such use, northern Peru's horses were large and not particularly refined in appearance. They were early developers who usually had heavy necks, docile natures, and comparatively less brio. In contrast to most workhorses, however, these multi-purpose horses also had extraordinarily smooth riding gaits; the best of them displayed spectacular termino.

In the early 1900's significant northern bloodstock originated from the Haciendas Pucala and Cayalti, two enormous northern sugar plantations, and from Federico de la Torre Ugarte's famed Hacienda Palomino. Over the years important contributions were also made by Anibal Vasquez, Jorge Juan Pinillos and the Zapata family.

Though the Hacienda Casa Grande produced hundreds of horses, these animals constituted a separate type of horse altogether, and until the 1960's these lines played a relatively small role in the affairs of the modern Peruvian Paso horse.

SOUTHERN PERU

In contrast to the large agricultural areas of the north, the southern Peruvian coast is an extraordinarily dry ribbon of land. Some desert coastal regions in southern Peru have received no rain for hundreds of years. The saving grace for agriculture in southern Peru is the many canyons (*quebradas*) formed by small rivers that flow down the western slopes of the Andean mountains and empty into the Pacific Ocean. Along the coast, where rivers enter the ocean, are oasis areas, or small fertile sections of land. Southern Peru's haciendas are situated in these coastal areas.

It has always been impossible for southern Peruvian hacienda owners to produce the same kinds and quantities of crops as their northern cousins. Therefore, these establishments generally excel at growing crops---such as wine grapes—that require less space, more intensive care, and generate more income per productive acre.

The southern landowner needed an animal who could carry him surefootedly and comfortably over all kinds of terrain. These southern Peruvian

Horse breeders placed premium value on beauty, spiritedness and sure-footedness. Their horses generally possessed great brio, were very strong, and boasted the fine, luxurious manes and tails of their primary forebears, the Spanish Andaluse/Barbs and Jennets. They were also rather plain headed, like the Jennet. These southern horses were late developing, not always well locked in their gaits and in general possessed less termino than their northern counterparts.

Older Cansino and—it is believed by some—De Gregory bloodlines formed the basis for southern breeding programs managed by Gustavo de la Borda and Alfredo Elias. Though Fernando Peschiera was also a southern breeder so far as geography goes, he became best known for uniting the blood of northern and southern Peruvian Horses.

CENTRAL PERU

The geographic, cultural and political center of Peru is still the city of Lima. Lima and the immediate surrounding area is, therefore, considered central Peru. Central Peru is more commercial than agricultural, and is more densely populated than either the southern or northern portions of the country.

Horses from central Peru had light, graceful necks topped by pretty heads with large eyes and small, shapely ears. These horses were very well conformed, and had very well established saddle gaits. Horses from central Peru, however, often demonstrated less brio and termino than their southern and northern counterparts, and travelled with less grace and animation.

Important modern Peruvian bloodlines from central Peru were established by Jose "Pepe" Musante, Carlos Parodi, and Eugenio Isola.

During the 1920's the advent of the machine age nearly wiped out the Peruvian Horse. In 1923 Lima's streets were paved, and horses were prohibited from coming into the city. Most breeders followed the trends of the day, and sold out their best stock, usually for a pittance. But a small group of central Peruvian breeders conscientiously preserved the best bloodlines of the area so they would be available to future generations. Some of these men were Mario Canepa of the Hacienda Puente, Dr. Hugo Magill of the Hacienda

HEAVENLY GAITS

Nana, Pio Delgado, Carlos Ravina, Jose Antonio Dapelo, Sr., Ernesto Nicolini, and Manuel del Solar of the Hacienda Vasquez. The Hacienda Pando, owned and managed by a number of men, was at the forefront of the movement to preserve the best central Peruvian bloodlines.

COMMON QUALITIES OF THREE TYPES

Despite the differences in their horses, all Peruvian Horse breeders valued certain qualities in their stock: brio; termino; good pisos (smoothness and quality of gait), a fine hair coat; long, flowing manes and tails; great strength, endurance and energy; and refinement of features. But for many years geographical isolation, and pride, prevented breeders from the three regions of the country from crossing their bloodstocks to create one breed of horse that would consistently display an outstanding degree of all of the ideal characteristics. Though all Peruvian Horses, because of common ancestry and patient, knowledgeable breeding practices, possessed most of these traits to one degree or another, no one type of Peruvian Horse was strongly imbued with all of the desirable characteristics.

ESTABLISHING A SINGLE TYPE OF PERUVIAN PASO

Not until the 1940's did breeders from the three regions of Peru begin to collaborate in their efforts to produce a single type of horse to fairly and consistently represent the national breed. This collaboration was aided by the efforts of Carlos Luna de la Fuente, a Lima businessman and professionally trained animal husbandman. Luna de la Fuenta, who became well known within breed circles, was one of the first men to possess some technical knowledge and understanding of the Peruvian Paso. Later on other men like Jose "Pepe" Musante, Ecuadorian author Luis de Ascasubi and judge and breeder Fernando Grana would add significantly to this store of knowledge.

In 1942 Luna de la Fuenta opened La Agricola, Lima's first agricultural supply store. Shortly thereafter Peruvian Horse breeders from all over the country, lured by Luna de la Fuenta's knowledge as well as by his extraordinary hospitality, began to congregate regularly in a back room specifically set aside for this purpose at the La Agricola. Many important breeders from the three regions of Peru were brought together for the first time by Carlos Luna at the La Agricola. These introductions were the forerunners of horse trading, purchasing and breeding deals—and of the exchange of accurate technical information---that would be monumentally important to the improvement and prosperity of the Peruvian Paso breed.

THE FIRST MAJOR NORTH-SOUTH CROSS BREEDER

Fernando Peschiera, a southern breeder, was one of the first major breeders to cross regional lines after he made a buying trip to Federico de la Torre Ugarte's Hacienda Palomino. Peschiera was set upon purchasing some top quality horses to begin what was to become the country's first major cross breeding of north-south horses. After a full day of evaluating and riding different horses, Peschiera selected seven of Federico's de la Torre Ugarte's mares for purchase. One of the mares, a graceful chestnut with high white socks by the name of Lujosa, was in foal. After finalizing the agreement to purchase the horses, Peschiera asked Ugarte what stallion had been used to sire Lujosa's foal. Upon checking the farm's breeding records Ugarte discovered that she had been bred to Carnaval, a son of Limenito, one of the breed's greatest sires. Though don Federico immediately regretted having sold an excellent mare so bred, there was no way at that point to honorably back out of the deal. Lujosa, and the foal she carried, would belong to Fernando Peschiera.

Peschiera himself was especially delighted with the deal. Years before he had seen Carnaval at a provincial horse show and been so impressed by the young colt that he'd tried, unsuccessfully, to purchase him. Now he would own one of the stallion's get, by a mare whose line the knowledgeable horseman respected.

This was to prove an even better deal for Peschiera than even he could have imagined at that point. The foal out of Lujosa was a filly named Silvana. Silvana grew up and gave birth to El Cid, three time Peruvian National Champion of Champion stallion. (Champion of Champion designates a horse who has won a special competition among the current and previous National

Champions.) Lujosa and her daughter Silvana provided Peschiera with a number of other National Champion—and Champion of Champions—offspring, giving his breeding operation a solid foundation upon which to build.

Peschiera also purchased breeding stock from Jorge Juan Pinillos and Pedro Cabrera. Peschiera's foresighted efforts paid off in the flesh of extraordinarily fine Peruvian Paso horses. These animals were, for all practical purposes, hybrid animals. Such hybrids are less prepotent—or likely to consistently produce quality, true to type offspring—than line-bred animals because of their genetically diverse backgrounds. Individual hybrids, however, are often outstanding since they possess the best qualities of each parent. Once good strong crosses have been made, prepotent types can later be established through successive generations of line breeding the hybrid's best offspring.

Fernando Peschiera's contribution to the welfare of his beloved Peruvian Paso was dramatically celebrated at the 1980 U.S. National Championship show in Santa Barbara, California when he was the beneficiary of a surprise presentation called the "El Cid Presentation." As Peschiera stood in the center of the show arena before a large crowd, U.S. breeders and owners exhibited some of El Cid's finest offspring for him, many of which Peschiera had never before seen, as they had been imported to the U.S. *in utero*.

CHANGING TRADITIONS

This presentation was especially appropriate in light of the fact that the cooperative endeavor begun by Fernando Peschiera was fueled by the sudden popularity of the Peruvian Paso horse with people from the United States, who began to export them in appreciable numbers during 1960's and 70's. Prior to this time hacienda owners had taken their horses for granted, casually giving away or lending good animals to friends and relatives, selling them for token sums, and breeding mares to top quality stallions for little or no cost. Though good horses were important in themselves, making a profit from horses was of little concern to these men, since farming was their primary money-making venture. The main thrust of all Peruvian breeding programs was, besides the pleasure to be gained by associating with good horses, to produce good working farm stock. Smooth riding, strong geldings—and excellent quality mules—were the most highly prized animals on the Peruvian hacienda.

Increasing demand for the smooth riding Peruvian Paso created by the U.S. export market gradually changed the major Peruvian breeders' way of thinking. Also, the Agrarian Reform made large-scale breeding prohibitively expensive, so that those who wanted to continue breeding horses had to now finance their activities through the sale of animals and stud services. Jose Antonio Otero once explained, "I do not breed horses in order to be able to sell them. I sell horses in order to be able to breed them." After the Agrarian Reform, this became true for most breeders. During this time the value of breeding quality horses—and the ever-diligent Peruvian horseman would allow nothing but premium quality horses to be used for this purpose—escalated dramatically.

NATIONAL PERUVIAN PASO ORGANIZATION

Though provincial horse shows had long been popular in Peru, it wasn't until 1945 that the first National Championship Show was held in Lima. This came about largely because most of the major Peruvian Horse breeders were for the first time in close contact with one another. These men recognized the increasingly important role horse shows played as a forum for their top quality bloodstock.

The first two Peruvian Paso National horse shows were held under the auspices of Peru's Club Hipico, a highly respected national horse organization. Members of this club, however, were more familiar with trotting sport horses than with Peruvian Pasos. For this reason, in 1947 the Asociacion Nacional de Criadores y Propietarios de Caballos Peruanos de Paso (ANCPCPP) was formed. As Verne Albright, the breed's preeminent U.S. historian and promoter tells it, the first ANCPCPP meeting was held at Carlos Luna's La Agricola. Under the light of a kerosene lamp, using a bale of hay for a table, thirteen men signed a paper that had been written by a lawyer, Fernando Fernandini, upon a piece of wrapping paper. This paper described the

HEAVENLY GAITS

purposes of the new organization. The original thirteen founding members of the ANCPCPP were Carlos Brazzini, Ernesto Carozzi, Fernando Fernandini, Santiago Gerbolini, Alfredo Gonzalez, Carlos Gonzalez, Eugenio Isola, Carlos Luna de la Fuente, Oswaldo Llorens, Jose Musante, Carlos Parodi, Jorge Juan Pinillos and Federico de la Torre Ugarte.

HORSES OF DESTINY

Fernando Peschiera's purchase of Lujosa and the subsequent events leading to the creation of the stallion El Cid, who was undefeated in the show ring, might be viewed as serendipitous by some. But many people who trace the origins of outstanding breed sires eventually come to the conclusion that the events leading to the conception, discovery and/or use of such horses must surely be guided by a Sovereign hand. True stories relating to two of the Peruvian Paso's most prepotent sires could easily lead one to this conclusion.

LIMENITO'S TALE

The first story involves the events leading to the conception of Limenito, a prepotent stallion who was not only grand sire to El Cid, but whose get dominates the Peruvian Paso show rings and breeding sheds until the present day. It seems that northern breeder and cattle baron Andres Zapata had one of his farm hands journey out with an important message to a distant hacienda. On his way back home, the messenger stopped at Ugarte's Hacienda Palomino and exchanged his tired Zapata horse for a fresh mount graciously offered by Federico de la Torre Ugarte. Upon arriving back at the Zapata farm after dark, the messenger turned the Ugarte horse loose in a field before retiring.

Early the next morning one of Zapata's sons spied this strange horse foraging upon the precious pasture his father had carved out of the Peruvian desert, and promptly shot the animal dead. When the family discovered that this dead horse had not been an opportunistic intruder, but one that Federico de la Torre Ugarte had lent to his father's messenger, they chose one of their most promising young fillies to send to Ugarte, with apologies.

The Zapata mare sent to don Federico was La Zapata, who went on to become Peruvian Champion of Champions in 1946, and produced many important sons and daughters. By far the most significant of these was Limenito, who was produced by crossing La Zapata with Ugarte's Limeno Viejo (by Pin Pin), a stallion said to originate from southern Peru. Limenito was not only destined to become the most important foundation sire for the Hacienda Palomino, but his blood became the major influence undergirding the breeding of the northern Peruvian Paso breeding operations. Limenito's blood became instrumental in the upgrading (through integration of north, central and south animals) of all Peruvian Paso horse bloodstock. Limenito breeding is still an important cornerstone upon which rests the contemporary Peruvian Paso horse. De la Torre Ugarte, whose breeding program depended upon Limenito, was so highly esteemed for his fine bloodstock contributions to the breed that he was awarded lifetime honorary Presidency of the ANCPCPP.

SOL DE ORO (V)

The cornerstone laid by Limenito blood is not the most important foundation stone to today's Peruvian Paso. The one horse who can truly be said to be the greatest Peruvian Paso sire of all time was southern Peru's Sol de Oro Viejo. (Viejo means "The Elder," and will henceforth be designated as [V].) This horse might well have lived out his life as a crippled scrub horse in the mountains of southern Peru, had it not been for a man by the name of Gustavo de la Borda. The discovery and subsequent use of Sol De Oro (V) is another of those stories that could convince a breed historian that there must be an element of Sovereign planning in equine affairs.

In the early 1920's Peru, along with the rest of the world, entered the Machine Age. When the Panamerican Highway came through Ica in the 30's, southern Peruvians' need for good riding horses was further diminished. Since southern haciendas were much smaller than their northern counterparts, farmers of that region were easily able to replace the horse with modern equipment. Unfortunately, this was the area known for the finest Peruvian Paso bloodlines—most notably those lines cultivated by don Jose Cansino of

HEAVENLY GAITS

Palpa, a breeder by the name of Arriola, from Pisco, and one-time Peruvian President Domingo Elias.

Once horses became little more than a hobby, the majority of southern farmers sold their stallions and brood bands. Though some horses remained in the coastal areas, only a very few men still practiced careful, selective horse breeding. Many of the horses sold went cheaply into the hands of peasant farmers with lands located in the canyons, or quebradas, of southern Peru. The rough mountainous terrain of this area still required the use of horses. The geographical isolation of the quebradas ensured that the southern bloodlines were preserved, and even intensified through line breeding—though the size and condition of the horses declined as a result of casual care and poor nutrition.

GUSTAVO DE LA BORDA

Gustavo de la Borda was a son of Jose de la Borda, one of the few southern Peruvian men who still valued fine horses during this period. Upon his father's death Gustavo inherited his father's horses. At about this time horse shows were becoming popular, and it was a great disappointment to Gustavo de la Borda—and other southern breeders—that all of the top prizes of these competitions went to breeders from northern and central Peru. This was a hard pill to swallow for these horsemen, as in the past southern Peru was well known for producing the best Peruvian Pasos in the country.

Gustavo de la Borda gradually came to the belief that many of the bloodlines that had been lost to southern breeders were still conserved in the quebradas. Fueled by this belief, Gustavo began traveling up and down the mountain canyons in search of good bloodstock to bring back to his farm on the coast.

GUSTAVO'S DISCOVERY

On one of these journeys Gustavo discovered a stallion who was in sorry shape. One foreleg had been broken when the horse was roped from a mountainside field at the age of three years. The limb had healed crookedly, and caused the horse some pain. The stallion was considered worthless by his owners, since he couldn't be ridden; therefore he had received very little attention or care. The current owner couldn't tell how old the horse was, from what quebrada farm he originated, or who had been his sire. Such facts seemed irrelevant to the farmer, especially when considering such a sorry specimen of horse flesh.

But Gustavo de la Borda's practiced eye told him that despite outward appearances, here was a stallion with great potential. He was especially impressed by the tremendous amount of brio displayed by the small, damaged horse. Dispensing with the usual dickering that usually precedes a horse sale, he paid two hundred dollars for the crippled animal. The farmer who sold Gustavo the horse considered this buyer to be crazy, or an idiot—and not a few of Gustavo's peers in the horse breeding business agreed with this assessment, once they saw the stallion Gustavo brought out of the mountains. They ridiculed him for using such a stallion on his mares, and one prominent judge referred to the horse as "a strong box on legs." Only two other breeders, Jose "Pepe" Musante and Alfredo Elias, Gustavo's brother-in-law, shared his enthusiasm for the damaged stud.

Gustavo was known for outstanding generosity. If another man particularly admired one of Gustavo's horses, it wasn't at all unusual for him to give the animal to him, regardless of its value or beauty. Under just such circumstances he once gave a stallion named Caramelo to Alfredo Elias. Caramelo (by Sol de Oro [V] and out of Sultana) went on to become Peru's Champion of Champion's three years in a row. Many times Gustavo arranged for his top stallions to be delivered to other haciendas for extended free services to the property's mares. He once said that he was especially gratified that "anyone who has ever wanted my blood, has had it."

So it was to be expected that, besides Gustavo de la Borda, Pepe Musante and Alfredo Elias would now be the first recipients of the services, and offspring, of Sol de Oro (V), the new addition to de la Borda's stable—and they were. After Pepe Musante's first crop of foals from Sol de Oro (V), however, his enthusiasm was tempered for a while, and he gelded the only male among them. But Alfredo Elias, Gustavo's brother-in-law, never lost faith in the stallion. As the show ring success of Alfredo Elias's horses began to amply substantiate Gustavo's high opinion of Sol de Oro (V), breeders from all over Peru requested, and received, his services and get for their breeding programs. It was largely due to don Gustavo's outstanding generosity that the prepotent stallion sired so many fine horses during the time that was left him---though that was plenty of time, as the best estimates as to Sol de Oro (V)'s age put the hardly little stallion at thirty years when he died.

Gustavo de la Borda's wisdom in rescuing this horse from his mountainside prison has been proved over and over again through the years. Every National Champion of Champions in Peru since 1961 has carried Sol de Oro (V)'s blood; it has also flowed through every U.S. Champion of Champions since 1973.

In April, 1969 the *Asociacion Nacional de Criadores y Propietarios de Caballos Peruanos de Paso* honored three men with solid silver replicas of the traditional Peruvian stirrup in recognition of their contributions to the modern Peruvian Paso Horse. One went to Federico de la Torre Ugarte for the excellent foundation breeding stock he contributed to the northern breeding farms; another was awarded to Luis de Ascusubi for his contribution to the growth of technical knowledge; yet another was awarded to Gustavo de la Borda for having given the breed some of its most significant horses—by far the most influential of these was the great Sol de Oro (V).

PASSIONATE PROMOTER

Though a number of men have played significant roles in popularizing the Peruvian Horse in North America, one man, Verne R. Albright, stands—at 6' 9" tall, literally and figuratively—head and shoulders above the rest. Albright has personally arranged for the sale and importation of a number of excellent quality horses from some of Peru's top breeders. This was no small feat of salesmanship and diplomacy, since for many years the

Peruvians considered their horses to be a kind of national treasure, and were loathe to export good breeding stock. It is largely thanks to Albright's efforts that the Peruvian Horse continues to exist as anything other than a rare breed, since the 1960's Peruvian political upheavals seriously endangered most of the major breeding operations. Breeding farms in the U.S. and Canada helped ensure the horse's long-term prosperity.

Verne Albright himself has written several hundred articles and a number of books on the subject of the Peruvian Horse; this author and others regard these as the most important English language research information available on the breed. Albright once undertook a remarkable journey from South America to the U.S. He rode Peruvian Pasos the entire way, and afterward penned a book about his adventures, *Horseback Across the Americas*, which further helped to promote the breed.

PERUVIAN PASO'S PHYSICAL CHARACTERISTICS

The Peruvian Paso stands between 14.1 and 15 hands. A horse with sufficient brio—proud spirit under control—may give the impression of greater size. This breed comes in nearly every possible solid color, including bay, chestnut, brown, gray, black and dun. White markings on the face and below the knee and hock are accepted, as is dappling. White on the legs above the knees are considered a fault, and not desired in breeding stock. Spots are also considered undesirable—though there is a (rare) tendency among the Arriola and a few other bloodlines for white spots to appear on the saddle area. This is known as the *lomo nevado*, or snow covered back.

The Peruvian Horse has good, clean bone, with legs approximately as long as the body is deep. The hind legs are well angled. He has a short back, great depth through the body, and is strongly coupled through the hips and loins. The neck is of medium length and sets high into a very sloping shoulder. His head is very attractive, with sharply chiseled features, the ears small, and the eye large and expressive. A distinctive feature of this horse is that he exhibits a very high head carriage, as though always on parade. Peruvian Horses have fine hair coats, with luxurious and long manes and tails. The tail is attached low and carried tucked in.

Photo courtesy of Mrs. Mac Clabaugh

This well-conformed Peruvian Paso Horse is performing the sobreanado, a very fast broken pace.

The Peruvian is an exceptionally strong horse. As a comparison to the English term "horsepower," which indicates the amount of power required to pull 33,000 pounds one foot in one minute. Peruvian breeders, whose horses aren't driven, coined the phrase "Peruvian Horsepower." It was long ago decided by those who shaped the breed that a horse with sufficient "Peruvian Horsepower" is one that can carry 220 pounds over 30 miles of ground in five hours. A "round trip horse" is a paso who can make such a trip both ways in a little over twice the time.

Photo courtesy of Mrs. Mac Clabaugh

Traditional Peruvian Paso headgear includes the Jaquima (halter), and Tapa Ojo (leather, diamond-shaped blinders). Usually crafted of finely-braided leather, and heavily silvered, the entire headpiece may weigh up to 18 pounds.

HEAVENLY GAITS

PERUVIAN TACK

Just as the ancestry of the Peruvian Horse goes very deep, so do the traditions regarding his trappings. The style of tack still commonly used on the Peruvian Paso today originated in the 16 century, when equestrian pursuits were raised to the level of art.

THE HEADGEAR

A Peruvian Horse's headgear consists of three parts. The primary part is the bridle and reins. In some cases a bozal is used rather than a bridle, depending upon the horse's age and level of training. The *Jaquima* is a halter with a long lead attached, and is used to longe the horse before the rider mounts. The most unusual element of the Peruvian Paso's headgear is the *Tapa Ojo*, which consists of two diamond shaped leather patches worn on the forehead above the eyes. These can be pulled down over the horse's eyes, and are used to keep a young horse calm when he is first mounted, and as a means of anchoring a horse on the treeless Peruvian desert. Since a horse who can't see won't travel far on his own, Peruvians came up with this ingenious device to prevent their horses from wandering away when they had to leave the animal's side. Most good Peruvian headgear is made of extremely soft, fine leather strips expertly braided in traditional patterns. This tack is heavily silvered, so much so that the entire headgear can weigh as much as 18 pounds. It takes a very strong horse to easily carry his head high under such weight.

THE SADDLE

The Peruvian saddle's design is amazingly similar to the way saddles appear in Renaissance era paintings. Short and compact, it has a high pommel and cantle and square skirts. The leather skirts have graceful hand-tooled designs, and intricate silver workings. The older traditional Peruvian saddle had very narrow bars, and was sometimes criticized as being uncomfortable both for the horse and for the rider. Most modern-day Peruvian saddle makers have modified the saddle's design and underpinnings to provide a more comfortable fit for both, while maintaining the traditional look.

Photo courtesy of Mrs. Mac Clabaugh

Traditional Peruvian tack including headgear, saddle, guarnicion and pyramid-shaped stirrups. Also shown is lady's Peruvian style side-saddle.

HEAVENLY GAITS

Stirrups are pyramid shaped carved wood, solid on three sides, with a toe hole carved into the fourth. These are easily detached from the stirrup leathers. Stirrups like these were truly multi-purpose, useful items to early Peruvian riders. Besides offering excellent protection for the rider's foot, they could be detached and used as a formidable weapon, as a candle holder, or as a cup for a drink of water. When buried in the sand and attached by a stirrup leather to the horse's halter, this stirrup made an impromptu anchor.

THE GUARNICION

Another unique aspect of the Peruvian Paso's gear is the *guarnicion*, leather trappings or tracings worn about the horse's hindquarters. These include a crupper, decorative tail cover, and retrancas, leather straps that loop around from just behind the cantle down past the horse's hocks and attach under the saddle skirts at the sides. Again, the idea for such tack probably originated in the 1600's, when the Spanish hung tapestries and other decorations about the rear quarters of the horse. Though the guarnicion serves no real purpose, it is employed as a matter of tradition.

MAINTAINING A VALUABLE TRADITION

Of course anyone owning or riding a Peruvian Paso may elect to use any kind of tack they prefer. Often these horses are ridden in western or english tack in the U.S., and most large Peruvian shows, especially in the U.S., include ladies sidesaddle classes. It's important to understand, however, that the traditions associated with the Peruvian Paso horse go back hundreds of years. Anyone who values a horse with such a rich heritage would naturally be very careful in their efforts not to contribute to its decline. Owners and breeders of Peruvian Paso horse are the caretakers of an animal with perhaps the most direct, unbroken line to ancient equestrian history.

TRADITIONAL PERUVIAN PASO TRAINING METHODS

As with nearly everything associated with the Peruvian Horse, the training methods commonly employed up until the present have their origins in the Renaissance era, when equestrian pursuits were raised to an art form.

A riding master named Frederico Grisone, a nobleman from Naples, founded the world's first riding academy in Italy. Men came from all over the world to study under his tutelage. In 1550 Grisone published *Gli Ordini de ca Valcare*, a book outlining his philosophy for and methods of horse training. It is obvious from this book that Grisone had carefully studied the works of Xenophon, a Greek statesman and diplomat whose equestrian book, *Hippike*, written in 400 B.C., is the earliest such work to be preserved and passed down. In some instances Grisone quotes Xenophon word for word.

Pignatelli, a student of Grisone's, went on to become the Director of the Riding Academy in Naples. One of his students was Frenchman Antoine de Pluvinel, who became riding master to Louis 13th. Some of Pluvinel's methods laid the foundation for the classical training of the Peruvian Paso horse.

Xenophon introduced the idea of working horses around a pillar, or pole, but the method fell out of use after his time. Pluvinel reintroduced the pillar as a systematic means of conditioning and training a horse. Basically, the horse is initially longed around a single pole; much later on he is taught to perform High School maneuvers between two stationery pillars. Pluvinel says of the pillar's use:

> *"By continuing with these lessons three important things are achieved; first, they never get strong in the mouth; second, they are never restless; third, they rarely turn stubborn or willful or resist turning to the right or left which is the most common fault one finds in an unschooled horse."*

Judiciously working a horse around a pole does have the effect of suppling the horse's body while conditioning his mind toward obedience. A Peruvian Paso riding master, called a *chalan* (cha-lan', the first 'a' is hard), uses this method to make his horse remarkably supple and cat-like in his movements, and minutely obedient to the rider or handler.

On the other hand, this kind of training is sheer torture for the horse if overdone or performed inappropriately. For this reason some North American trainers dismiss such training as cruel. We should remember that, as with most horse-related endeavors, a method or device is generally only as harsh as the person using it.

The *bozal* that is used in the early training of Peruvian Pasos is quite like the type originated with Grisone. Though he employed harsh bits in his training, these were introduced when the horse reached maturity. In order to avoid "marring the mouth" of a young horse, he used a leather cavesson, secured under the chin, with reins attached to the top of the noseband. Though most bozal trainers today attach reins under the horse's jaw, the Peruvian Paso's traditional bozal still has the reins attached over the horse's nose.

Even a bozal, however, can be and is sometimes misused. Grisone eschewed harsh use of the device, and instructed horsemen to handle a horse so equipped gently, so that he is neither physically injured nor fearful. He also taught that: *Neither must you use any other kind of bridle than this. . .until your horse can trot clear, keep the ring, stop and turn roundly on both hands."*

The chalan follows this advice, waiting until the horse is four or five years of age before introducing a bit. As was advocated by Renaissance trainers, the bit is first introduced with the bozal reins still in place, and another set of reins attached to the shanks of the bit shaft. The horse is then worked off four reins, with more and more emphasis being placed upon the bit reins until he is working strictly from the these. At that time the bozal reins are removed. Traditionally, even finished Peruvian Horses are taught to work off a direct rein.

The well-trained Peruvian Horse's initial lesson usually teaches him to double, that is, to bring his head back to his rider's calf in a willing, soft fashion. This suppling of the horse enables him to work the circles and spirals that are then introduced. These follow set patterns, each lesson or pattern becoming more challenging than the last.

The highest achievement of Peruvian Paso training is a form of High School riding called *enfrenadura*. The enfrenadura is a complicated, subtle form of riding that was practiced by top-notch chalanes, and originated as a way to train horses for the "Suerte Nacional," or bullfighting ring. In exhibition, these graceful moves are often performed to music, and it looks as though the horse and rider are dancing. Though there are still a few chalanes practicing in North and South America, they have become rare; as a result, spectators will seldom see the enfrenadura performed in the Peruvian Paso show arena today.

PERUVIAN PASO GAITS

The Peruvian Paso gaits are the paso llano, the sobreandando and the huachano. The paso llano and the sobreando are both variations of the stepping pace, with the latter being faster and slightly more lateral in action than the former. The hauchano is a true pace.

Horses with excellent *thread* make smooth transitions from the flat walk all the way through the spectrum of gaits. A horse with *pisos* demonstrates gaits with good timing, extension, animation, elegance, smoothness and forward motion, or "advance." Some horses are said to have a *gateado* (cat-like) way of going. Horses with gateado are remarkably smooth and supple, and transmit literally no motion through their backs to their riders.

PERUVIAN TRAINERS

Until a horse is ready to be ridden, at about 2 1/2 years of age, the animal is taught by a *paleador*, a trainer who specializes in ground-work. When this training has sufficiently prepared the horse for work under saddle, training is continued under the guidance of a chalan.

The chalan was perhaps the most highly valued and respected employee of a Peruvian Horse breeder. Though the Peruvian Horse's gait is natural, teaching the horse to perform his gait and other traditional maneuvers at national competition level requires someone with a special talent and many years of experience. Trainers with such abilities used methods known only to themselves and the brotherhood of chalanes. There was during the 1940's and 50's a tight group of talented chalanes who were instrumental in gaining international recognition for the top breeders of Peru, and for their horses.

Two such men, Pedro Torres and Ricardo Soltero, both worked for four or five years at the Casa Grande. Both men learned their craft from Pedro's father, also named Pedro, who had acquired his knowledge from two black brothers by the last name of Ripalda. Pedro Torres, Jr. went on to train horses at the famed Pucala Hacienda. He became one of its principle trainers, and was acknowledged to be a master trainer—a designation bestowed only upon

171

the best of the best.

Torres' chum, Ricardo Soltero, also became a master trainer and worked for such highly esteemed men as Federico de la Torre Ugarte, Eugenio Isola, Pedro Cabrera and Fernando Peschiera.

Enemicio Caceda, a black man, was master trainer for many years at Casa Grande. His methods influenced many others who practiced the trade, including Sixto Chavez, a master trainer who went on to practice in the U.S. and Canada. Caceda's family boasted many trainers, including his nephew, Santos Plasencia. Santos worked as a *quebrantador*, or horse gentler, in Paijan. The important breeder Anibal Vasquez recommended him to Fernando Peschiera, who hired him to work at his hacienda in Chincha. Santos eventually became a trainer of Peruvians Pasos in the United States.

One of Federico de la Torre's master trainers for many years was Pedro Briones. Briones stayed on at the Palomino after Federico's death. When the Hacienda Palomino was confiscated by the government during the Agrarian Reform, Briones became head trainer at the Hacienda Cayalti.

It has been argued among aficionados of the Peruvian Paso that a man named Juan "Juanito" Bautista Orbegoso was the most gifted chalan of modern times. He was the equitation teacher for men such as Carlos Luna de la Fuente and Carlos Parodi. Juanito worked for many years for Pepe Musante, who said of him, "He had a rhythm with horses that distinguished him completely from ordinary mortals." At eighty years of age, Juanito Orbegoso died while riding one of Musante's horses in a parade.

When the top breeding farms in Peru disappeared or were sadly diminished after the Agrarian Reform, a number of chalanes journeyed to horse farms in North America to practice, and teach, their craft. There are some such men still working on Peruvian Paso farms in North America. Unfortunately, people from the United States have been raised in a culture where faster is often considered better, and few possess the wisdom to appreciate the slow, painstaking and patient methods employed by Peruvian chalanes. We too often expect our horses to be ridden at two years of age, and "finished" by three. This kind of thinking, and the training shortcuts it demands, has resulted in a decline in the number of people practicing the traditional methods of training Peruvian Paso horses. Where such methods are still practiced, we will still find the Peruvian Paso horse exhibiting the fullest degree of the remarkable beauty, grace and willingness for which it is known.

THE PERUVIAN PASO SHOW

Peruvian Pasos up to the age of three are shown in halter, and the chalan who exhibits these animals must be in excellent physical shape, as he must run alongside the horse in order to demonstrate its natural gaits for the judge. Three and four year old horses may be shown in bozal classes. After the age of four or five they are exhibited "under saddle and in the bit." At this age,

Riders of Peruvian Pasos dress all in white.

the chalan may also opt to wear spurs. Horses are shown at the walk, the paso llano, and the sobreando. Horses are never asked to canter or run, except in the enfrenadura.

Because the emphasis is on horses with a natural four-beat gait, the Peruvian Horse is shown without shoes, or any other artificial devices. Riders, exhibitors and all show officials, except the judge, dress entirely in white—white jeans, long-sleeved shirts, white neck scarves, and white straw hats, or sombreros. White or earth-colored ponchos are worn in all but bozal saddle classes. Originally white apparel was worn to refract the hot Peruvian desert sun from the rider's body. Later on the showman wore white in order not to attract attention from his horse. One final piece of gear now so expensive that it is rarely seen outside the show ring is the *pellon*, a soft braided wool pad fitted over the seat of the saddle. The pellon was originally used to protect the rider's white clothing from travel dust.

In the U.S. there are Pleasure, English, Western and Sidesaddle show classes where colorful attire is allowed. But even here, in deference to tradition, flashy show clothing, rhinestones and ruffles are taboo in the show ring.

In Peru show horses never enter the show cold, but under the supervision of show officials are ridden six to ten miles—depending upon gender—before their classes begin. This practice effectively eliminates horses suffering from subtle lameness, and those who possess insufficient endurance or brio. The horse's endurance is further tested in the show ring. Classes, divided by age and gender, can last an or more hour each. A Peruvian Paso judge is very deliberate in his examination of each horse. He often asks the opinion of other knowledgeable people, and may ride one or more of the top contenders to evaluate their gait and smoothness for himself. When he has finally reached a decision, rather than simply announcing the winners, he sometimes details his reasons for choosing each horse. Primary emphasis, as always, is placed upon choosing horses with characteristics that will improve the breed.

Mares with young foals are shown with their foals walking alongside them around the ring. This not only eliminates the anxiety associated with separation—thus allowing the mare to show to her best advantage—but allows spectators a chance to view show ring contenders of the future performing

Judy Frederick photo, courtesy of Rancho de Colores

Elegancia MSR and her foal, Galantino MSR, show foal gaiting perfectly alongside dam. Such show ring appearances of dam and foal are common, and great crowd pleasers.

their natural gaits alongside their dams.

Both in Peru and in the U.S. horses that earn the title "Champion of Champions" for three years are retired from competition. Such retired horses are honored with the title Laureado (for stallions) or Laureada (for mares).

PROMINENT PERUVIAN PASO HORSE SHOWS

The National Championship Show for Peruvian Pasos in Peru is held each year in Lima. The U.S. National Show is held varying locations all across the U.S. In addition to these, at the time of this writing shows are being held in Canada and at least 20 states in the U.S. The popularity of this breed is quickly increasing, and it is likely that before long Peruvian Paso horse shows will be common in every state of the U.S.

For more information regarding shows, interested parties should contact either of the two U.S. Peruvian Paso registries listed in Appendix C.

HEAVENLY GAITS

OTHER USES FOR THE PERUVIAN PASO

Most Peruvian Horse aficionados make no claims about their horse being the most versatile of breeds, but readily admit that they are, above all else, an excellent riding, parade and exhibition horse. The Peruvian Paso seldom, if ever, competes in dressage, hunting/jumping or driving events.

Besides being used for pleasure trail riding and show, the flashy, proud Peruvian Paso is an excellent parade and drill team horse. He is also gaining a reputation as a good competitive trail horse. This is understandable, as the Peruvian Paso's speed, endurance, sure-footedness, obedience under saddle, courage and comfortable riding gait makes him an ideal mount for long rides over difficult terrain. Those who participate in field trials—where people hunt game birds from horseback with the aid of dogs—have found that most Peruvian Horses get along with the dogs, are smooth to ride, navigate easily through brush and woods, do not spook at gunfire, ground tie well when needed, and catch on to new tasks quickly. This horse's short stature, docile nature and extraordinarily smooth riding gait make him a popular choice for use in handicapped riding programs. Elderly people, or anyone whose riding is limited because of physical problems, may be delighted to discover they can comfortably ride the smooth gait of the Peruvian Paso—and without fear of falling, since he is usually a well-mannered, sure-footed and "bomb proof" animal.

While it cannot be claimed that this horse is a "jack of all trades," thanks to hundreds of years of selective breeding by the most patient of men, those things that the Peruvian Paso does, he does very well indeed.

—Chapter Seven—
The Paso Fino

The Paso Fino is not so much a single breed of horse, but a group of several types of horses, each issuing from a different country but sharing similar ancestry and ancient history, and several important characteristics. The most significant common characteristic among the various basic types of Paso Fino horses is their smooth saddle gait, the paso fino, a short-stepping broken pace for which the breed is named and from which it takes its primary standard.

The Paso Fino has been developed from strains of horses bred and raised on the West Indies islands of Cuba, Puerto Rico, and the Dominican Republic, and in the South American country of Colombia. Each type was developed in their respective countries from bloodstock originating prior to the mid-1500's from the South of Spain—and therefore all share the noble blood of the Spanish Andaluse/Barb and the more common-appearing ambling Spanish Jennet (or *Genet de'Espagne*).

Because of this incredible diversity, it would be impossible to go into a detailed history of the background of every type of Paso Fino horse. For our purposes, therefore, we will cover a very broad general history, and then "zero in" on the history and type of Paso Fino that is being bred in the United States—also known as the American Paso Fino.

HEAVENLY GAITS

EARLY ORIGINS OF THE PASO FINO

Christopher Columbus was responsible for importing the first horses to the New World in 1493, when he brought horses to Hispaniola (now the Dominican Republican) for the purpose of establishing a remount station for Spain's conquest of the New World. Other such horse breeding operations were soon established on the islands of Cuba and Jamaica. Columbus convinced Queen Isabella of the importance of sending only the finest bloodstock to these state-operated horse breeding stations.

From these remount locations horses were sent to Central, South and North America, where they enabled Spaniards to conquer these lands for the Spanish crown. By the mid-1500's, however, mother Spain's horse stock was sorely depleted. All exportation of horses to the remount stations ceased, thereby decreasing the amount of new blood entering the horse population of each country. There were, however, crosses made to English horses at various times through the years. It seems likely, for example, that the Paso Fino horses of the Caribbean Islands carry blood from the Narragansett Pacer, as these early American horses were imported to the West Indies from the English colonies in large numbers during the 1700's. In an effort to increase the size of their Paso Fino, Puerto Rican breeders once experimented with crossing them to Tennessee Walking Horses. At various times English settlers crossed their cobs, drafts and warm-bloods to the island horses.

VARYING TYPES DEVELOP

Over the years horses from Cuba, Puerto Rico, the Dominican Republic, and Colombia each took on unique characteristics as a result of the climate, geography, and breeding and cultural practices of their new homelands. Between the years 1550 and 1900 horses from the West Indies tended toward a common standard, while Colombian horses tended toward another. Though frequently it's been claimed that Colombian Paso Finos are larger, the primary difference between the strains isn't size so much as it is variances in gaits and differences in conformation. Colombian horse breeders, whose horses were often used for rugged mountain travel, weren't as strict about their horses maintaining a true stepping pace; consequently, their horses tended to move between gaits. Puerto Rican horses were a great deal more controlled in their action.

One problem that the entire breed suffered from was too many poor quality horses, overall. A long-standing Latin American belief that all men should ride stallions often resulted in inferior males being kept whole. Often such horses were used to breed mares—*any and all* mares— which predictably resulted in lower quality offspring. It also had the effect of maintaining a very large gene pool, thereby producing many unrelated lines of horses with unpredictable breeding qualities. Despite this, there have always been conscientious breeders of Paso Finos in every country from which the horse originates. These breeders, like breeders of fine horses everywhere, were very exacting in their standards.

Colombian Paso Fino horses began to be exported in significant numbers to the Dominican Republic in the 1970's. This infusion of Colombian blood tended to improve the quality of Dominican Paso Finos—but not because the Colombian horses were better. Naturally, only excellent quality horses were imported for breeding, which gave Dominican breeders the chance to choose from a wider variety of quality bloodstock, both imported and domestic. Importing enabled them to cross their native horses to obtain qualities that were somewhat lacking in their particular strain of Paso Fino. At the same time, the Colombian horses also benefited from these crosses, as their offspring inherited qualities that were more strongly present in the Dominican horses. Dominican Republican breeders, in short, had the best of both worlds at their disposal.

Puerto Rican breeders were less enthusiastic about crossing their horses with Colombian stock, and for good reason. Colombian horses weren't as "true gaited" as Puerto Rican stock, and these conscientious breeders were reluctant to do anything that might cause a decline in their horses' gait. For a time this placed them at a disadvantage at international competitions—but over time the Puerto Rican Paso Fino has proved itself to be equal to any.

Two types of Paso Fino horses, both proud, elegant, powerful and pleasing to the eye. Above, Festival Doc Bravo is owned by Sharon Cochran; below, Centauro la estrella is owned by Carolyn Bloxsom.

Photo by Dan Bouray, courtesy of 4-Beat magazine

Photo courtesy of Carolyn Bloxsom

THE AMERICAN PASO FINO

Beginning in the late-1950's and early 1960's, people from the U.S. began importing Paso horses from Puerto Rico, Cuba, the Dominican Republic, Peru and Colombia, with the majority of early stock originating from Puerto Rico. True to their cultural inclination to blend bloodstocks to create something entirely unique, many U.S. breeders crossed these varying types of Paso Fino horses—and an occasional Peruvian Paso cousin—to create a particular type of Paso Fino. In the United States The Paso Fino Horse Owners and Breeders Association was formed in 1973 to represent this "old breed of new horse." The registry's name has since been changed to Paso Fino Horse Association (PFHA).

FOUNDATION SIRES

In 1974 the new U.S. breed registry designated six stallions—originating from three different countries—as foundation sires. This was done in response to many inquiries from broodmare owners, who wanted to learn what to look for in a good Paso Fino stallion, and where to find such horses. Each stallion chosen was considered to be the epitome of a well-built, finely gaited, refined and talented Paso Fino. Though each possessed excellent quality and gaits, they varied in type. Regardless of the type, each of the following foundation sires was known to consistently pass his superb qualities on to his offspring.

MAR DE PLATA LaCE

Mar de Plata LaCE was a gray stallion from Colombia who eventually turned pure white. He was sired by Vinol out of La Urbana, and traces three times to Resorte I and twice to Carey, both outstanding Colombian Paso Fino sires. Mar de Plata possessed a very pure gait, refined but substantial conformation, and extraordinary intensity and energy. His breeder, German Posada Angel, did not use the stallion for showing or breeding in Colombia, but in 1969 George J. LaHood, his U.S. owner, campaigned this extraordinary horse to the U.S. First Grand National

Champion title. (LaCE—pronounced La-say— stands for LaHood's Champion Equines, and is a suffix to the names of horses who have been imported or owned by George J. LaHood, Jr., an important breeder and knowledgeable promoter of American Paso Fino horses.)

Mar de Plata LaCE sired black, gray and bay horses who tend to possess his intensity, beauty and gaits. One of his sons was Manolito LaCE, the first U.S. Grand National Champion of Champions in 1973, and that year's Horse of the Year. He was also sire to an all-time great show mare named Marlena LaCE. Mar de Plata sired so many outstanding show horses that he consistently placed high on the breed association's annual list of top ten sires. This honor is given to stallions whose offspring garner the greatest number of National show points during the year.

BOLERO LaCE

In 1968 Mr. LaHood imported the Puerto Rican stallion Bolero LaCE to the U.S., where he was used by Paso Fino Farm, Inc. as a breeding stallion. Bolero was by the renowned Puerto Rican stallion Volare, and out of the dam Morena. Both his sire and dam were also brought to the U.S., where they have made important contributions to the breed.

Bolero LaCE possessed a remarkably balanced conformation, a gentle nature, excellent gaits, and a long, luxurious mane and tail. He had already sired a few truly outstanding show horses in his native land, though due to a serious case of founder it was thought the black stallion himself could not be shown. After intensive treatment, however, he made a remarkable recovery, so that by 1969 Bolero LaCE was named National Champion Classic Paso Fino and National Champion Conformation Paso Fino. He went on to win many other such honors, as well as to become sire to several other significant offspring. One famous Bolero LaCE offspring is Marichal, the 1973 and 1974 National and Grand National Champion in Conformation, 1974 National and Grand National Champion in Classic Fino and 1974 Reserve National Champion in Versatility and Western Pleasure. More recently, his son Campesino LaCE and grandson Bravado Windsong have been shown to top National honors. This helps to demonstrate how Bolero LaCE's contribution to the breed doesn't stop with his sons and daughters, but are transferred to the third and fourth generations of American Paso Finos.

FAETON LaCE

Faeton LaCE was a striking bright red chestnut with golden eyes. He was foaled in 1956 in Puerto Rico, the son of a famous four-time Island Champion named Guamani. His grand sire was perhaps Puerto Rico's most famous sire, Dulce Sueno. Faeton's dam was Piel de Seda, a mare with strong Andalusian breeding. Faeton earned many awards on the island, including the 1960 Horse of the Year Award.

Faeton was imported into the U.S. in 1964, and went to live in Oklahoma, where at the time there were few opportunities for showing or exhibiting Paso Fino horses. George LaHood, Jr. purchased Faeton LaCE in 1970, and in 1971 sold him to Drs. John and Carolyn Ziegler, from Ohio. That same year Faeton LaCE was named the APFHA Sire of the Year. In 1973 he was again honored with that title, and was one of the registry's top ten sires in 1978—at 22 years of age.

EL PASTOR

El Pastor must have a "lucky number" of five. The foundation sire El Pastor is the only horse to have won the breed association's "Sire of the Year" title five times. This blood red bay, who was imported from Colombia in 1967 as a four-year-old, also traces to the famed Paso Fino sire Resorte five times.

El Pastor was Grand National Champion and Horse of the Year in 1972, and Grand National Champion in 1973. He holds National Championships in versatility, conformation, performance, costume, equitation, western pleasure and Paso Fino pleasure.

El Pastor is especially fiery in temperament, which resulted in his being consigned to a public stock horse auction after he was brought to the U.S., where Henrietta and Robin Ratliff purchased him. Though difficult to handle—some believe he was treated roughly as a youngster—El Pastor's conformation is second to none. This world-class stallion's conformation, bold carriage, excellent pure gaits and electrifying presence is consistently passed on to his sons and daughters. He is the only sire of the breed ever to have had a National Champion son or daughter in every Paso Fino show horse class division—conformation, fino, performance, pleasure, versatility, trail, driving and agility. One El Pastor daughter, Dali Sin Par, tallied up more National Show points than any other Paso Fino horse in the nation, living or dead.

HILACHAS

A Colombian horse named Hilachas was foaled in the mountains of Colombia, and always retained the spirit of freedom and remarkable intelligence such an early start imparts. Hilachas was imported to the U.S. in 1968 as a twelve-year-old. Since then his offspring, and grand-offspring, have won more than 150 Grand National Championships, in addition to many dozens of other prestigious titles and awards. A gray mare, Erectora Que tal, is probably the most celebrated of these.

Hilachas was named Sire of the Year in 1974, 1975 and 1976, indicating that his offspring won more National show points than those of any other American Paso Fino stallion. His abilities and prepotency was passed on, as he and his sons and daughters have consistently placed among the registry's prestigious list of Top Ten Sires and Dams.

LUCERITO

Though last on this list of American foundation sires, Lucerito is anything but last in quality among the six—and his story is perhaps the most fascinating. Lucerito once belonged to General Trujillo, of the Dominican Republic. In June of 1961 the General was assassinated, and people of the Republic began to riot soon thereafter. Just before fleeing the country with his family, the commander's administrative officer released the General's horses and chased them up into the mountains, where they would be safe from rioters. There Lucerito lived as a feral stallion with his band of brood mares.

A few years later, after the government was once again stable, there was a great deal of interest in capturing the famous stallion. After several failed attempts, Lucerito was finally captured. Shortly thereafter, despite his still wild ways, he was shown and named National Champion of the Dominican Republic. At that show Mildred and Marlow Jacobsen, from the U.S., saw Lucerito and made arrangements to purchase him for their string of Paso Finos near Homestead, Florida. They never suspected that the horse who seemed so mild in his stall at the fairgrounds objected violently to being ridden!

It seems Lucerito also objected to being transported to the U.S. by air. During the trip, despite being tranquilized, he broke several halters and escaped from his large shipping box three times. The pilot of that chartered plane had the authority to have the horse killed, as he was a danger to the plane—and he very nearly had to use that authority. The exit from the plane was nearly as dramatic as events during the flight.

Eventually Lucerito was removed safely from the plane and taken to his new home in Florida. Though he never did enjoy being ridden—and forcefully demonstrated his objections at every opportunity—he was easy to handle from the ground. His saving grace was that he proved to be very enthusiastic about breeding mares. In fact, every time Lucerito left "his" farm and "his" mares he dropped up to 100 pounds of weight very quickly. This resulted in his early retirement from the show ring—though his presence can be seen in the American Paso Fino show rings to this day. He was named Stallion of the Year twice, and is sire and grandsire to many National and Grand National Champions.

OTHER IMPORTANT INFLUENCES

Since the main purpose for designating American Paso Fino foundation sires was to aid broodmare owners, only stallions still alive were considered for the honor. Stallions who were deceased at the time of selection, but who have had an important impact on American Paso Finos include Resorte, Dulce Sueno, Kofresi, Volare, Mahoma, Mariscalato, Muneco LaCE and Oasis Z. One or more of these stallions, as well as other sires and dams, may one day have their names added to the list of foundation blood stock.

The pool of U.S. Paso Fino blood was never limited to foundation sires. There continued to be numerous importations of excellent bloodstock into the U.S. Dominican imports were particularly sought after in the U.S. during the 1980's. In 1983 a Dominican import, La Marqueza de Besilu, won U.S. Grand National Championship titles in the Bellas Formas (conformation) and Classic Fino (gaited) divisions.

Breeders from the U.S. continue to import Paso Finos from their countries of origin for crossing to their quality U.S. bloodlines. There are also American breeders of Paso Finos who prefer to specialize in pure strains of Puerto Rican, Dominican Republican or Colombian bloodstock.

No matter where this breed of horse comes from, or what his particular type, he always brings his inbred "paso fino," or fine gait, with him.

185

CHARACTERISTICS OF THE PASO FINO

Bellas Formas is the term used to refer to the conformational makeup of the Paso Fino. Loosely translated this means "exciting or pleasing form". This is generally true of the breed. Paso Finos are proud, expressive and spirited. They exhibit plenty of *brio*, or controlled spirit. The beauty and grace of their Andalusian forebears is still evident in their carriage. A good Paso Fino is exciting to watch, symmetrically built, and pleasing to the eye. It gives the overall impression of great grace, presence and power.

This breed ranges between 13.2 and 15.2 hands, with 14.2 being the average height. Thanks to the great variety of blood in its heritage, these horses come in a rainbow of colors, with or without white markings on the body, face and legs.

The Paso Fino should possess a fine head with large, softly expressive and widely spaced dark eyes—no white should show at the edges. The muzzle is tapered and finely sculpted, ending with good-sized, very dilatable nostrils and a generous, firm and expressive mouth. Ears are short, and often curve inward at the tips. The Paso Fino's medium length neck is set high into a very long, sloping shoulder. The neck may appear slightly heavy, but should always be supple and well-arched. The forelock is long and full, falling over the horse's face; the mane is luxurious, wavy and long with fine silken hairs, again like its Andalusian forebears.

The Paso Fino should not possess extremely bulky musculature, but should give the impression of having powerful, smooth and well-rounded muscles all over. The chest is deep, the ribs rounded, the withers well-defined but not prominent. The back should be straight or very slightly concave, and of medium length and width. There should be smooth rounded coupling at the loins. The croup of the ideal Paso Fino demonstrates a sloping pelvis line, with a rounded rump. An abundant, medium-long tail is set on slightly low. The horse should be as deep through the loins as it is through the heart girth, with the bottom line slightly longer than the topline.

The legs of a good Paso Fino are straight and refined, with strong, clearly defined joints and tendons. The pasterns are medium to long, and have about a 45 degree angle. Feet are relatively small, with a low heel.

GAITS OF THE PASO FINO

The distinctive gait this horse has been bred for is the *paso fino*, or fine walk. This unique gait is essentially a broken pace. The manner of its execution, however, is unique to the Paso Fino. Ideally it is performed with great collection, fully balanced, and with plenty of drive or impulsion from the hind quarters. The horse takes very rapid but short steps, and there is little extension or forward advance. The horse must give the impression of great spirit and power under complete submission to and control of the rider.

The *paso corto* is also a broken pace, but performed with less collection, slightly more extension and a bit longer stride than is the paso fino. This is usually the Paso Fino's best traveling gait.

The *paso largo* is the fastest form of this breed's inborn broken pace gait. The horse's stride and extension are much greater than in the other forms of gait. It's been claimed that a horse performing paso largo may travel at speeds up to 16 miles per hour.

In addition to the paso fino, paso corto and paso largo, the horse should possess a relaxing, free-style walk, and may or may not canter. Some horses may fall into the pace, the *trocha*, or the *trocha y galope*. The first is a true two-beat lateral gait, the second a four-beat diagonal gait, and the latter a mixture of two-beat diagonal interspersed with canter. The latter two gaits may be comfortable to ride, particularly over hilly terrain where they were originally developed. But any of these less-than-pure gaits are considered serious show ring faults, and are grounds for disqualification from a class.

TRAINING THE PASO FINO

The Paso Fino who will be used for pleasure and performance classes is trained much the same as any other horse, with the exception that the trainer must be very familiar with the horse's working gait, the paso corto. Even the horse being readied for Classic Fino classes may be started much the same as any other horse—but it takes an experienced Paso Fino horse trainer to develop a potential Classic Fino show horse's gait to its finest degree. Improper training of such horses may result in animals who don't correctly

The horse above demonstrates the paso fino gait. Below, Rosalie MacWilliam rides Brita Conchita in a paso largo. Brita Conchita is a mare by the Puerto Rican Island Champion Batalla, by foundation sire Dulce Sueno.

differentiate between gaits, or who pace and/or trocha. Worse, poor training of the fino gait may cause the horse to perform his gait with little drive and poor execution—some people have likened the appearance of such a horse to that of a lifeless puppet dangling from a string.

Usually trainers of these horses progress from working with pleasure horses to training performance horses. After they have had ample experience with these, and once they've found an experienced teacher, they may move on to training the Classic Fino horse.

There is now a movement among breeders, owners and trainers in the U.S. to concentrate on producing performance horses, either in addition to or rather than breeding and training Classic Fino horses. Performance horses are not required to execute the extremely rapid, short-stepping paso fino gait, which in some circles has been faulted as being detrimental to the overall long-term heritable strength and well-being of the Paso Fino. Such a view holds that breeding for an extremely short stride results in horses with significantly less overall strength, ability and practical value. Also, these people point out, the Classic Fino gait is stressful, as the horse's foot lands on the ground many times more than it would were it traveling the same distance with a longer-strided gait. While performing the Classic Fino gait the horse's frame and muscles are kept in constant collection. Over time, some people believe the stress caused by such physical demands may contribute to founder or other mechanical breakdowns of the horse. Some American breeders particularly resist breeding a horse for shortened stride, since lengthened stride has always been the ideal standard for U.S horses.

It should be noted that traditional Paso Fino breeders object strenuously to these arguments. They point out that it is the Classic Fino gait that has always distinguished their horse from all others in the world, and that their breed tends to be extremely robust and sound. A compromise is now in the making: many breeders strive to produce horses who are able to collect and extend, to move with either long or short strides. Such extraordinary horses can compete both as Classic Fino horses, and as performance horses.

Carolyn Bloxsom shows Centauro la estrella while wearing traditional formal Paso Fino show ring attire.

TACK AND APPOINTMENTS

The Paso Fino is traditionally ridden with a flat english (Saddleseat), english all-purpose, or english dressage saddle, an english style bridle with cavesson, curb bit and chin chain. Western tack is used in western pleasure classes, and is also often seen on the trail. The only type of saddle not permitted at P.F.H.A. sanctioned shows is the "forward seat" english, or jumping saddle. Silver on the saddle—whether english or western—is allowed but must not be excessive.

Mane and tails are kept long and natural, though a bridle path of no more than four inches is allowed. Horses may be shown bare-foot or flat-shod, but cannot be exhibited with weights, pads or other artificial devices. Breast collars are allowed if a horse performs a jump in english tack, and in western classes. Tie-downs, draw reins and martingales are prohibited. Riders may carry short riding crops and wear blunt spurs.

Official Paso Fino show attire includes a long-sleeved bolero jacket, and riding pants with a full-width lower cut to accommodate boots. The shirt or blouse is moderately ruffled, and worn with a string tie. A Spanish felt hat is worn by male riders, and may be worn by women—though any exhibitor may opt to use a safety helmet. Cummerbunds are usual, but optional.

In western show classes the usual western show attire is worn.

AMERICAN PASO FINO HORSE SHOWS

There are approximately 110 shows sponsored each year by the Paso Fino Horse Association. These are held in every region of the country. A few of the larger, more prominent shows are listed below. For information regarding shows in your region, or the current locations of some of the shows below, contact the PFHA.

The Nationals Horse Show is the PFHA's premier show, and is held in differing locations of the United States. Other big shows are: the Spectrum, in Ocala, Florida; the State Fair of Florida; Southern Regional Paso Fino Extravaganza; Kentucky Horse Park Paso Fino Show; Latta Plantation Show in Charlotte, North Carolina; Paso Finos at Griffith Park, Los Angeles, California; The 4-Beat Jubilee held in the Southwest; and the Syracuse, New York show.

TYPES OF PASO FINO SHOW CLASSES

There are many types of classes at Paso Fino shows. The Paso Fino Bellas Formas is a conformation class, where horses are judged on gait as well as conformation. Exhibitors in Bellas Formas must show their horse performing either the Classic Fino or the paso corto at the end of a lead line, or with two handlers and two lead lines.

In the Classic Fino class, horses are shown performing only the Classic Fino gait. Performance classes require that the horse show at the walk, paso corto, and paso largo.

The Versatility class requires the walk, paso corto, paso largo, and canter. In addition, the horse will be asked to perform various maneuvers, including jumping, various figures, and backing.

Paso Fino Pleasure classes require horses to move through the walk, paso corto and paso largo in a relaxed manner, and greater stress is placed on manners than on gait.

Western classes require the walk, paso corto and lope, and the horse must present the image of a classic stock-type horse. Walk and paso corto are the only gaits required in Trail classes, where the horses are ridden through a set of from six to eight obstacles. Either English or Western attire is allowed, though it must be comfortable and appropriate to a trail class. Judges in this class may, or may not, specify what gait the horse is to use in any given maneuver, and canter or lope is allowed during jumping phases.

Equitation class participants are expected to ride the horse using a deep, balanced seat, and be in complete control at all times. Equitation competitors must ride their horses through the walk and paso corto, and some of the latter gait must be ridden without benefit of stirrups. Riders must back the horse, dismount and mount, and ride through a figure eight at paso corto. They also will be quizzed to determine their knowledge about points of a horse, and tack.

In addition to the above, Costume classes give exhibitors the opportunity to dress themselves and their horses up in costumes employed in their countries of origin. Get of Sire and Produce of Dams classes are held during National competition, where horses are judged by the typiness and quality of their offspring. The National Show also offers a Pleasure Driving class, Youth classes, Schooling classes for young horses, and a Gelding Futurity.

IMPORTANT BREED PROMOTERS

There have been a great many Paso Fino enthusiasts who have helped this horse gain popularity, both in the U.S. and abroad. Each year the PFHA awards one such outstanding individual its Merit of Honor award (now called the Rosalie MacWilliam Merit of Honor Award) for their tireless efforts on behalf of the Paso Fino horse. So far, people receiving this honor have been: Rosalie MacWilliam, Carolyn Karnes, Dr. Carolyn Ziegler, George J. LaHood, Jr., Winona Walton, Dr. Maurice "Bud" Hirsch, Alvaro and Clemencia Iriarte, Jackie Bailey, Rita Magaha and Charles D. Minter, Sr.

FUTURE OF THE PASO FINO

The Paso Fino is an extremely popular horse in all the countries of his origin, as well as in the United States, where it has enjoyed unprecedented growth. In 1990 there were just 16,213 horses registered with the PFHA. That number grew to 22,394 by 1994—an increase of nearly 40% in just four years! These numbers help explain why many horse people who breed, import or purchase horses for investment purposes are interested in the Paso Fino. This kind of growth, however, can bring its own problems. Potential owners of Paso Finos should be certain they are purchasing quality stock from reputable, knowledgeable people.

Recently people from other nations have become interested in this breed of horse, and a Paso Fino charter association was recently formed in Mid-Europe. The ongoing efforts of people like those named above, combined with the natural beauty, smooth gaits and versatility of the Paso Fino horse assures this breed a prominent place in the hearts and lives of horse-loving people the world over.

The Paso Fino—as fun and useful on the trail as in the show ring!

—Chapter Eight—
Other Gaited Horses

Besides the breeds already written about in this work, there are a number of other breed associations that register various types of gaited horse stock. Though many of these Associations are relatively new, they all share a common vision: the official registry and improvement of a particular type of gaited horse. This chapter will give information about several of these associations, their histories, goals—and horses.

RACKING HORSES

In the 1960's Harold B. Blach, Jr. of Birmingham, Alabama began to notice that "There was this horse being shown in great numbers, a horse of a distinct type and characteristics, for which there was no specific judge, no show ring category, no organization and ultimately no incentive for expansion and growth." At the time, Blach and another man, Joe D. Bright, were in 50/50 partnership on several Tennessee Walking Horses. Always a man of both vision and action, Blach determined to do something for those horses, and their owners, who he felt deserved more official recognition.

As a result, the Racking Horse Breeders' Association of America was officially formed on May 23, 1971. Owners of horses who could perform a natural racking gait were invited to register their animals with this new organization. Many of the first horses thus registered came from the (registered and non-registered) ranks of the Tennessee Walking Horse. Saddle-breds and various types of other high quality horses were also accepted into the registry. The first president of the RHBAA was Joe D. Bright of Helena, Alabama.

Decatur, Alabama is the "seat" of the Association. With more than 12,000 registered Racking Horses, Alabama has declared this breed the official State Horse of Alabama. But the Racking Horse is not limited to Alabama. There are currently 70,000 horses registered with the RHBAA. These are located in every state of the U.S., as well as in Canada, Germany, Australia and the Netherlands.

From the beginning, Blach, Bright and other Association founders believed three things were important to the continued success of this type of horse. The horse must have a natural racking, or single-footing, gait, and never require the use of action devices. Secondly, the horse must not be required to canter. Also, they believed it must not show with a set tail.

The objective of the RHBAA was to create a market within the economic reach of middle-class Americans, who do much of their own training and showing. Through the Association such people would be given an opportunity to own stylish, registered Racking horses at reasonable cost. There would be approved stallions and mares for them to choose from in their breeding programs. And, perhaps most importantly, these amateur horse people would have a place to show their horses, where both they and their animals would be treated with respect.

Racking horses are a light horse, standing an average of 15.2 hands with a weight of around 1,000 pounds. They are gracefully built with long, arched necks, full-flanks, substantial frames, finely textured hair coats, and proudly held tails. They may be black, bay, brown, sorrel, chestnut, gray, yellow or spotted in color.

Currently the RHBAA qualifies regional commissioners who can examine and qualify horses for registry, based on their quality, type and gaits. The registry's long-term goal is to close their books to outside blood by the year 2,000.

The Spring and World Celebrations are held annually at the Southeastern Sports Arena in Priceville, five miles east of Decatur, Alabama. The RHBAA also sponsors a futurity, and an annual Racking Horse sale. Racking

Horses are always shown with english tack and appointments, but within these guidelines there are a great many classes and divisions. At both the Spring and World Celebrations—as well as at RHBAA sanctioned shows throughout the U.S—there are usually classes for naturally shod horses, as well as for horses shown with pads. There are many divisions, including classes for driving, pleasure, park, trail, youth, versatility and style. The Spring Celebration is a four day event, and the World Celebration, which started in 1972 as a one-day event with 257 horses—now features over 600 horses and is scheduled over a nine-day stretch each September. Racking horses have proved to be very popular: over 75,000 people now travel to Decatur, Alabama each year in connection with the Racking Horse World Celebration.

(As of this writing there is a new Racking Horse breed Association forming—please see Appendix III for name and address if you desire more information.)

THE SPOTTED SADDLE HORSE

Spanish American type spotted ponies were crossed with other gaited horses—with a preponderance of Tennessee Walking Horse blood—to produce a naturally gaited, spotted horse that combines the gentleness and tractability of a pony in a horse large enough for adults. These horses—like most breeds with pinto coloration—have burgeoned in number over the past several years.

There are two breed registries that represent these remarkably popular horses. The Spotted Saddle Horse Breeders' and Exhibitors' Association (SSHBEA), and the National Spotted Saddle Horse Association (NSSHA).

Spotted Saddle Horses of either Association must be naturally gaited, and exhibit pinto coloring,. The Spotted Saddle Horse is usually exhibited under western tack. Both breed associations sponsor shows, and the number and types of classes are nearly limitless: these horses may may be shown in Trail, Model, Light Shod and Open, Breeding, Pleasure, Halter, Driving, English Pleasure and Youth classes. There is a growing interest in stock-type show events (roping, barrel-racing), as well as the usual age and gender divisions.

197

Spotted Saddle Horses are stylish show ring contenders. Above, Bridge's Battle Cry competes in Open Shod class, ridden by Freida Bullard, owned by the Boyd Elliot family. Below, My Sippin' Whiskey demonstrates his outstanding barrel-racing abilities as a Competitive Stock Horse. He is owned and ridden by Virginia Lally.

Spotted Saddle Horses, besides being stylish and fun to show, are excellent trail and family pleasure horses. Because of their calm dispositions, easy gaits and sure-footedness, these are popular Bird Dog Field Trial horses. Like the Paint Horse, these spotted equines are enjoying tremendous popularity, which means that they are presently a good investment. The NSSHA numbered only 715 registered horses in 1990; that number was over 10,000 in 1994—over a *ten-fold* increase in just four years! Likewise, the SSHBEA has demonstrated remarkable growth, with over 2,600 members and 14,000 horses registered, up from just 4,600 horses in 1990.

NORTH AMERICAN SINGLE-FOOTING HORSE

According to Barbara Bouray, President of the North American Single-Footing Horse Association (NASHA), this organization was formed in January 1991: . . ."by members of an all-gaited horse trail-riding club. Almost all gaited breeds were represented in this club, yet it was found that when people talked about their all-time favorite trail horse, they listed exactly the same qualities in virtually the same order of importance. They also mentioned that very often they had to breed a different kind of horse to win in their breed show ring—often ones with exaggerated gait or another quality. And often they found themselves selecting for qualities that were at odds with the qualities they found so desirable in trail horses.

"NASHA was formed to develop the ideal long-distance travel horse based on what riders who had logged thousands of miles on gaited horses consistently requested. Emphasis is placed on a natural, [even or] near-evenly timed 4-beat intermediate gait (road gait) that is easy for the horse to maintain on long rides over varying terrain. The ideal gait does not require careful training and riding to maintain, nor artificial devices to develop. Also desirable is a good range in gait speeds, maximum smoothness at all speeds, and a smooth transition from the walk to the road gait."

NASHA looks for a tractable, easy-to handle horse with enough energy to want to work; one with endurance, versatility and sure-footedness.

Horses registered with NASHA may be registered with other associations, or not, from gaited or non-gaited breeds, or result from custom crosses.

HEAVENLY GAITS

Many members are interested in crossing the Spanish blood breeds with the southern-style plantation and saddle horses.

This registry stresses usefulness and versatility in their program. Besides being used as pleasure and competitive trail horses, NASHA horses do everything from working cattle to performing in stylish Park Horse equitation, harness and side-saddle classes, to "Renaissance" riding---an exhibition of dressage-like moves performed by non-trotting horses.

NASHA is very zealous and efficient in its endeavors to educate people about what constitutes a genuinely well-gaited horse, and how to breed for these qualities. People involved with this organization do not deride the show-ring types of gaited horses and their owners, nor do they place undue emphasis on the undesirable characteristics that tend to crop up in some gaited breeds. Rather, NASHA continually focuses attention on the type of gaited horse that has, through many years and over thousands of miles, consistently proved to be as safe, comfortable, versatile and willing as it is beautiful.

THE ROCKY MOUNTAIN HORSE

In 1986 the Rocky Mountain Horse Association was formed for the purpose of maintaining a type of horse that had become popular in Kentucky's Rocky Mountains. Though this horse was well-known to horsemen of that region, some of its history is as much a matter of tradition as recorded fact.

This tradition has it that a Virginian family passed through the mountains of Kentucky sometime in the 1890's. While there they sold a stud colt to a native Kentuckian. This stud proved to be a popular sire of medium-sized, ambling horses who were as gentle as they were sure-footed. He also proved to be highly prepotent, as were his get, so that in spite of some early outcrosses to native horses, horses of this line consistently bred true.

How much of the above is true and how much is tale can only be surmised. Where this story surely becomes factual is when it relates the story of Sam Tuttle and Old Tobe. Sam Tuttle bred the popular ambling horses that were popular in Kentucky on his farm in Spout Springs, Kentucky, and used them for his work as the horseback riding concessionaire in the State Park. Tuttle's most treasured stallion, Old Tobe, in spite of being an excellent

Rocky Mountain Horse demonstrating the chocolate with flaxen mane and tail coloring that is prevalent within the breed.

breeding stallion, was so gentle, sure-footed and smooth to ride that Tuttle would place older people, small children and those who were especially timid riders on his back for rides through the park. Old Tobe put hundreds of such folks at ease, and brought them home safely, for most of his 37 years. Before his death in 1964, Old Tobe had also managed to become the most significant sire of Rocky Mountain horses.

This type of gaited horse is almost surely of early Spanish origin, which heritage is reflected in his conformation. He is very gentle, with a keen intelligence that is expressed through bold eyes and alert ears. He is medium-sized, standing from 14.2 to 16 hands high, with an average height of 15 hands. He has a loose, laid-back shoulder, wide chest, and balanced conformation. This horse may be any solid color, with or without white markings on the face and lower legs. Chocolate-colored horses with flaxen manes and tails are common, and is considered the most desirable color combination among Rocky Mountain Horse enthusiasts. Most of these horses are very sure-footed, strong, and possessed of great endurance.

201

HEAVENLY GAITS

Most importantly, the Rocky Mountain horse must demonstrate a natural ambling four-beat gait with no evidence of pacing. He should not be ridden or shown with any sort of action devices or shoe pads. Horses meeting these criterion are still being accepted into the Rocky Mountain Horse registry, which has experienced steady growth since its inception. The Rocky Mountain horse is a good trail, pleasure, show, or family horse. As of this writing, it is also a good investment, its numbers having doubled between 1990 and 1994.

MOUNTAIN PLEASURE HORSE

The Mountain Pleasure Horse Association was founded on March 22, 1989. However, horses of this particular breed have been documented in our country for the past 160 years. So strong is the evidence for their essential role in the history of America's gaited horses that in 1994 Kentucky Governor Brereton C. Jones declared the MPH as the "parent stock of all other American breeds." This horse is especially noted for its easy-going temperament, as well as a strong and comfortable intermediate riding gait. They range in color; besides the usual array of chestnuts, buckskins, bay, grey, black and roan, there are a number of "chocolate" horses, and a large (approximately 17%) number of palominos. Horses

Photo courtesy of Favorite Gait magazine

Left, the Mountain Pleasure Horse stallion Gobel demonstrates how tractable this breed of horse is by performing tricks for his owner, Paul Stamper.

are, by requirement, solid colors only, with a limited amount of white being allowed on the horse's body. Horses measuring less than 14.2 hands at the withers cannot be registered with the MPHA.

The MPHA publishes a monthly newsletter for members, and sponsors an annual MPHA Classic horse show, with over 30 classes, each year. Though stylish, the MPHA emphasizes that their horses are best proven in "real life" situations, such as a 100-mile event, or back-yard birthday party.

KENTUCKY MOUNTAIN SADDLE HORSE

Still another registry for "mountain type" gaited horses is the Kentucky Mountain Saddle Horse Association, founded by Robert Robinson, Jr. in 1989. Mr. Robinson is still the president of the KMSHA, and says their main goal is—and always has been—to register mountain-type horses that exhibit a 4-beat gait, good temperament and sturdy conformation.

"We don't have any 'big wigs' in our Association," says Mr. Robinson. "We want the horse to be the center of attention—this is all about the horse coming out the winner." To that end, the Association registers horses of any size or color—excepting spotted horses—that exhibit the desired gait and temperament characteristics. The horse may or may not be registered with another Association. KMSHA has examiners all over the United States and Canada, and welcomes inquiries from people desiring to register their gaited, gentle riding horses.

Currently, the KMSHA has 2,000 horses registered, with more than 500 members.

FLORIDA CRACKER HORSE

Like many other southern states, Florida has made a rich contribution to our country's horse heritage. The Florida Cracker Horse is a genuine national treasure, with roots that go far back in this nation's history. The horse adopted its name from the Cracker people who used them, and these people received their names from the loud cracking whips they used while herding and penning wily Spanish cattle. These horses are descended from the horses the Spaniards originally introduced to Florida, starting as early as 1521. Many of them escaped to become feral horses, and the process of natural selection has imbued them with good sense and exceptionally hardy constitutions. They adapted well to the Florida climate, and excelled as working cow ponies- -though they are adept at many other uses, as well.

The Florida Cracker horse is known for unusual strength and endurance, a strong herding instinct, quickness, and a fast walking gait. Many of them perform the running walk, while others are natural amblers. The latter is often referred to as a "Coon Rack."

Several Florida ranchers continued to breed these horses into the late 20th century. In 1984, John Law Ayers of Brooksville, Florida, who had been raising Cracker horses since 1930, donated his horses to the Florida Department of Agriculture and Consumer Services. This was the start of the state's Agricultural Museum and Withlacoochee State Forest Cracker herds. In 1985, Friends of Paynes Prairie, Inc. donated six Ayers mares and a stallion to the Florida Park Service. These horses were released on the Paynes Prairie State Preserve, where free-roaming Cracker Horses once numbered in the thousands. Thanks to efforts like these—and the ongoing breeding programs of horseman raising Florida Cracker Horses—this once nearly-extinct breed of Colonial gaited horse is making a comeback.

Fiddle, a Florida Cracker Horse (Ayers line) owned by Sam P. Getzen.

Photo courtesy of Favorite Gait magazine

McCurdy Horses doing field work—where they really shine!

THE McCURDY PLANTATION HORSE

The McCurdy Plantation Horse is another very old Spanish Colonial type of gaited horse that nearly died out in this country, but which promoters are bringing back into popularity and use. This horse originated in Alabama, and is named after the McCurdy family, who raised and popularized them. These versatile, smooth-gaited horses were especially popular among plantation owners. Following the civil war, many of these land owners, rather than give their good McCurdy horses to the Northerners, turned them loose. Like the Florida Cracker horse—certainly a close cousin—many of these animals became feral. Still others were given to black people, who were also given access to McCurdy stallions. It was, in fact, these families who were largely responsible for maintaining the gene pool of the McCurdy Plantation Horse.

Though like most of these types the McCurdy can be found in nearly every solid color, there is a predominance of grey within this breed. They are usually rangy, strong and athletic horses boasting keen intelligence and tractability.

At present a formal registry is being formed, with about fifty mares and a half-dozen stallions registered so far.

THE WALKALOOSA

The Walkaloosa Horse Association was formed in 1985 to register horses with Appaloosa background and color who demonstrate intermediate saddle gaits. The Appaloosa, thanks to its early Spanish origins, has long been known to produce an occasional ambling horse. In fact, the gait which became known as the "Indian Shuffle" was one of the characteristics that caused Native Americans to value the Appaloosa

Right, the stallion Quinta Joe exhibits the gait and one of the color patterns that makes him eligible for registry with the Walkaloosa Horse Association.

Photo courtesy of Janet Weber

horse so highly.

Unfortunately, there has been so much out-crossing of early Appaloosa stock to Quarter Horses, Thoroughbreds and Arabians—all trotting breeds—that the original intermediate gaits have been essentially lost to the Appaloosa breed.

The Walkaloosa Horse Association's primary goal is to maintain and enlarge the gene pool of gaited horses with Appaloosa characteristics. Registered Appaloosas who can single-foot are eligible for registry with the WHA. Unfortunately, there are few old-foundation bred ambling Appaloosas left in the U.S. For this reason the WHA allows the registration of Appaloosa-type horses who have had their gait characteristics strengthened by judiciously cross-breeding with blood outside breed lines. All Walkaloosas must perform a true 4-beat gait. For registration, horses must have Appaloosa coat pattern, or be out of two Appaloosa/WHA registered parents. This breeding produces a uniquely colored, long-strided, strong-gaited, gentle, sure-footed and extremely hardy horse.

THE TIGER HORSE

Still another registry for gaited horses with Appaloosa characteristics has recently been formed: The Tiger Horse Association. The folks behind this move intend to register 500 foundation stock horses, and then "close the books" to create a distinct breed.

The Tiger Horse will demonstrate a good, ground-covering intermediate gait, typical Appaloosa coat patterns, striped hooves, white sclera around the eye, etc. In conformation it will exhibit no exaggerated muscling—organizers are adamant that these horses not be another colored version of the American Quarter Horse. It should stand between 14.2 and 16 hands tall, with well-angled shoulders and pasterns. Though a new registry, the folks in charge seem knowledgeable about the type of horse they are looking for. They are also well-organized and zealous. It seems what they are attempting is to restore all the many fine qualities of the original Appaloosa. Traditionally these eye-catching horses were known for ruggedness and good temperament. They used to also be known for their "Indian Shuffle, " or comfortable single-foot.

Ramblin' Rythm exhibits "ghost" horse pattern that Tiger Horse officials believe pass on the traditional "appy" coat colorations.

Over the past few generations this has been largely bred out, as has the smoother, more compact body type. Many Appaloosa breeders aren't even breeding for the distinct coat patterns any longer! Restoring these qualities, while adding refinement, may well cause the Tiger Horse to become one of the big "up-and-coming" new breeds of gaited horse over the next few years.

FUTURE OF THE GAITED HORSE

Shortly after man first took on the challenge of taming wild horses, he discovered that one type of horse was more comfortable to ride than another. Gaited horses have been with us ever since. In recent years there has been a wide-spread resurgence in the popularity of these horses. As they become more commonplace, people will have the opportunity to gain first-hand knowledge about how comfortable, gentle, stylish and versatile these kinds of horses tend to be. These practical advantages make it a sure bet that gaited horses of every description will continue to increase in popularity, usefulness, and value, in the years ahead.

Who knows? We may be now witnessing a "riding renaissance" that will see the number of gaited horses once again rival that of their trotting cousins.

—Appendix I—

Some readers of this book will undoubtedly be interested in learning more about the genetic factors of gait. There is no one to my knowledge more qualified and able to teach the subject of gait genetics than Mr. Eldon Eady, who has studied the subject for over thirty years. Mr. Eady teaches seminars on the subject, has produced a videotape, and is in the process of writing a book. The material here has been reprinted, with permission from the author and some minor editing for length, from 4-Beat magazine.

—THE GENETICS OF GAIT—
by Eldon Eady

There are only two gene pairs that produce all the different gaits. These are the trot/pace pair and a gait gene pair that acts always as a main gene and sometimes as a modifying gene. The gait gene produces gait by modifying the patterns of dominance and by changing the way the trot and pace genes interact. Each foal receives one of the trot/pace pair of genes from each parent. It will also receive a modifying gait gene—or walk gene—in varying degrees of intensity.

The trot/pace pair are the easiest to understand, so we will talk about them first. They belong to a class of genes called qualitative genes. They regulate the quality or kind of characteristics in the offspring. The best known qualitative gene pair in horses is the black/sorrel genes that produce color.

HEAVENLY GAITS

These genes have a dominant/recessive relationship where black is dominant over sorrel. There are only three ways that these qualitative color genes can combine: black/black, black/sorrel, or sorrel/sorrel. Since the sorrel gene is recessive, only the double sorrel horse will actually be sorrel in color. The black/sorrel combination will always produce black, and you will not know such a horse has a sorrel gene unless it produces a sorrel offspring when bred to a sorrel horse. Such recessive genes can remain hidden for many generations before they reappear in a foal.

The trot/pace gene pair act in a similar but not identical manner in an ungaited horse. The trot is dominant over the pace. You will never see a trot/trot horse pacing. A trot/pace horse will have a strong predisposition to trot, but will sometimes pace, usually only as a foal. A pace/pace horse will have a strong predisposition to pace, but will almost always trot as a yearling, and even as an adult will occasionally trot or fox trot.

So far this is simple. But when a horse has one or two strong modifying gait genes the result is more complex. Gait genes belong to a class of genes that are called poly genes, or quantitative genes. Poly genes regulate the amount or strength of a characteristic. These genes produce such things as height, length, size, milking ability, speed, rate of hoof growth, and so on. There are no patterns of dominance or recessiveness in poly genes, only varying strengths of the same thing. The characteristics produced by poly genes are evident in every individual of the species (unless sex related), but in different amounts.

Let's take the milking gene for dairy cattle as an example. Each cow has two milk-producing genes, but there may be as many a one hundred different of these milk genes. If you breed a high-producing cow to a bull that has inherited weak milking genes from both parents you will get a moderately good producing female. This is because quantitative genes are additive; ie: the strength of the gene from one parent is added to the strength of the gene from the other. This determines the characteristics of the offspring.

So to summarize: qualitative genes are either dominant or recessive, and particular ones may or may not be present within individuals of a species. Poly, or qualitative, genes are neither dominant nor recessive, but are present in varying strengths within every member of a species.

Gait genes are a complex type of poly gene. The main function of these genes in horses is to produce the basic walk. All horses have them in varying amounts. In the ungaited horses they are so weak that they do not change the trot/pace, trot/trot or pace/pace pair. In gaited horses the gait genes are strong enough to interfere, or modify, the trot/pace genes. The result is spectacular and produces a wide range of different gaits.

There is only one kind of gait gene, but there may be as many as one hundred different strengths. Each different strength of gait gene, combined with the three different possible trot/pace gene combinations, produce the variations of gait seen in gaited horses.

Since the strength of the two gait genes (one contributed by each parent) are added together to determine the amount of gait modification in the offspring, you need strong gait genes from both parents to produce a properly gaited horse. The strongest gait gene from only one parent will only get you half way there. The horse with the strongest gait genes will be the one that maintains an even four-beat gait at the highest speed for it's trot/pace type.

Over the years many horsemen have recognized the direct link between the flat walk, and gaitedness. To prove that the walk gene and gait genes are the same thing we'll look at the walk of all horses. You don't have to look far before you notice that some horses have a very weak walk, taking short stumpy steps before breaking into a trot at very slow speed. Others reach out and stride much better, reaching a higher speed before breaking. Still others are excellent flat walkers, striding, nodding, reaching, using their shoulders, traveling fast but still maintaining an even four-beat rhythm. The walk is clearly a quantitative genetic characteristic that shows continuous variation from one extreme to the other.

Now let's take a look at the characteristic we call gait. You also don't have to look far before you notice there are some strong-gaited horses, and some weak-gaited ones. Some can travel 4 or 5 miles per hour at an even four-beat gait before breaking to trot or pace, some 8 MPH, some don't break at all but drift only slightly into fox trot or stepping pace before breaking into a canter.

This is because gait genes are walk genes. The basic walk is the "pure" expression of these genes. If the walk genes are strong they become modifying genes that interfere with the trot/pace genes to produce gait—they cause the horse to try to "hold" to a four-beat stride, rather than break quickly to a two-beat trot or pace. If the walk genes are too weak to modify, then the horse isn't gaited, but breaks quickly to a two-beat trot or pace from a flat walk.

Now let's look at the different combinations of Trot/pace—Walk/walk genes. For simplicity's sake we'll call the walk gene pair the modifying factor (modifier). For now we'll use the symbols (M) for strong modifier—two strong walk genes from each parent; (m) for weak modifier—one weak and one strong walk gene from each parent; and (0) for no modifier—one weak walk gene from each parent. The symbol for trot gene will be (T) and for pace it will be (p).

TYPE ONE (TT0)—Double trot, no modifier

This is one of the most common genetic types. The horse does nothing but trot and will break from walk to trot at a slow rate of speed. The basic walk is slow and stiff with tight, short strides and very little articulation or flexing. Shoulder movement is very limited. (Rough gaited at the trot.)

TYPE TWO (TTm)—Double trot, weak modifier

This is the fast walker of the trotting breeds. The horse drifts fairly quickly to a fox trot and then a two-beat trot. It doesn't show much head nod at the fox trot. The fox trot may be so close to a trot that you need slow motion video to tell it is four-beat. The modifier may be more common in the trotting breeds than we realize. (Smooth gaited, long-strided flat walker, strong trotter.)

TYPE THREE (TTM)—Double trot, strong modifier

This horse does an extended walk, a good running walk of moderate speed, a rack, a fast four-beat fox trot, and a two-beat trot. The fox trot will show a jerky kind of head nod. You will never see this horse pace, even as a newborn foal. He will be an athletic, good moving horse, but very obviously a trotter. With a lot of training it is possible to move his flat walk up to the range of the running walk, but the horse will always break into a trot at high speed. Shoeing for the running walk does not work very well because you have to put heavy shoes on the back and this creates too much lift in the hind—too much hock action. (Smooth gaited at all gaits including the two-beat trot. Well. . .let's say *relatively* smooth two-beat trot.)

NOTE: The five-gaited American Saddlebred is usually a type three and deserves mention here. The pace has been completely eliminated from the Saddlebred and the claim is made that the slow gait and rack are not natural gaits, but the result of training. Training alone could never produce the rack of the Saddlebred, but without training the (TTM) horse may never display that gait. He will have a strong predisposition to trot, and if just allowed to do so will never develop an intermediate four-beat gait of any kind. The same goes for the double pace/strong gait horse (ppM), except that such a horse will prefer to pace.

Conformation and temperament change the way gait genes work, and this is especially evident in the Saddlebred.

TYPE FOUR (Tp0)—Trot/pace, no modifier

This is the ideal horse for the Standardbred when both trot and pace gaits are required. It will either trot or pace, and never do an intermediate gait except the basic walk. Without training it may prefer to trot, but will do either gait with ease. It will break into one or the other gait at very low speed. Makes a poor Big Lick horse because, though it can pace, it trots too readily. You seldom get a horse with two very weak walk genes in the gaited horse breeds.

TYPE FIVE (Tpm)—Trot/pace, weak modifier

This is a dual gaited horse, common in the Walking Horse breed, but difficult to identify because training will mask the gait so easily. At moderate speed this horse will drift to a fox trot or stepping pace. With patience this horse is capable of a very good running walk. This is the type that must be started in training by flat walking. You fully develop the flat walk—taking months to do so if necessary—before asking for speed. Then you begin to extend that flat walk up into the range of running walk. As soon as the horse drifts you correct it. Eventually you will have a good quality walking Horse, but never one that can compete at speed. Speed is the acid test of the genetics of gait. Types three and nine are trained the same way, if lite shod.

TYPE SIX (TpM)—Trot/pace, strong modifier

In my opinion, this is the ideal Tennessee Walking Horse. As a foal this horse will either trot or pace, and even as an adult will continue to do so when in the pasture. It may experience some difficulty in sorting the gaits out when first put into training, but soon becomes a horse that can easily hold an even gait at speed. Because of this it is easy to push the horse into an extended running walk to develop length of stride and overstride, while still maintaining head nod without heavy shoes. When pushed at extreme speed this horse will break into a canter. It may drift a little to the pace or the trot, but not enough to be detected without slow motion video. The great horses from Midnight Sun, and back, were this type. The type six will be an athletic, loose-moving and well-balanced horse, but it should also be noted that the ideal gaited horse will have excellent conformation and temperament as well. Just producing a type six doesn't automatically mean you have show quality. These horses may not even display much gait until training begins. Midnight Sun didn't gait well until he was a four-year-old, but became a spectacular lite-shod horse.

TYPE SEVEN (ppo)—double pace, no modifier

A hard pacer. Never trots except maybe a stumble as a foal. A horse that can pace while grazing. Moves stiffly. It cannot be made to nod properly even with pads, weights, shoes, chemicals, training or alligator clips.

TYPE EIGHT (ppm)—Double pace, weak modifier

The ideal Big Lick horse. This horse holds the flat walk better than type seven, and will not show the sharp transition to pace, but rather a fairly quick drift through the stepping pace to hard pace. This horse can be made to trot, but only with extreme methods. It can also be used as a heavy shod plantation horse, but a stronger modifier is better.

TYPE NINE (ppM)—Double pace, strong modifier

The ideal heavy-shod plantation horse. This horse will sometimes do a trot in the pasture, but seldom as an adult and very rarely under saddle. Almost always shows ability to trot as a yearling. Squares up well with heavy shoes. This horse can even make a good lite-shod running walk with a lot of training, but can never handle speed without heavy shoes. Left barefoot, this horse will have only moderate head nod and become very racky at average speeds. If you

—Appendix II—
Shoeing the Gaited Horse

Sometimes gaited horses need some mechanical help before they are able to perform a good intermediate gait. What follows here is a simplified explanation of various shoeing techniques that work to enhance the gaits. The owner's best resource is always a farrier who is experienced at working with gaited horses; however, not all good farriers have had the opportunity to do so. This will give the owner and farrier a starting point. Always keep in mind that changes in hoof angle, shoe weights, etc. should be made gradually, and that a shoeing system that works for one horse might not work for another. It is best to keep things as close to natural as possible, as heavy shoes and exaggerated hoof angles contribute to unsoundness.

BASIC ANGLES

Though every horse is different, and must be shod according to its individual conformation and gait requirements, there are a few "basic" angles that the farrier may use to start out with if he/she is not familiar with gaited horses. According to farriers who specialize at shoeing these horses, the walking horse's "basic" angle degrees are 48 behind, 52 in front. The Missouri Fox Trotter's are 52 in front, 55-60 behind.

Please keep in mind that these are only the *most general guidelines*, and that using any kind of pat "formula," without carefully assessing the horse's individual needs, can be extremely detrimental. We only offer this information because we are aware that in many places there are farriers who have no experience at all with these horses, and who don't have a clue about how to start working with them. If given a choice, always choose a farrier who has experience with your kind of horse.

SHOEING A PACEY HORSE

To help cure the pace, you might try shoeing the horse heavier in front than in back—perhaps even barefoot behind. You might try a slightly longer heel in front, and try adding a "trailer" to the hind shoe. This will "slow down" the hind feet. Using a caulk is common practice, but reliable sources assure us that these really don't do much for the horse. As for angles, you may start out with 48 behind/52 in front, and adjust as you go along.

Many pacey horses have difficulty performing a balanced canter. A squared toe or rolled toe shoe on the back feet may lessen injury if the horse tends to cross-fire (strike himself while cross cantering). Protective quarter boots on the front are a necessity when riding such a horse. Also, horses like this tend to have big back ends, and cannot be ridden as slowly as horses with tighter "hind ends." Let him move right out, and see if that doesn't make a big difference.

SHOEING A TROTTY HORSE

For the horse that trots more than desired, you can do exactly the opposite from above. On the front try a light shoe, a high angled heel and short toe, again with the same 48 behind/52 in front angles, to start. Hind feet have a longer toe and shorter heel angle, and carry a heavier shoe. Horses shod this way may tend to slip on pavement; you can increase traction with a small heel calk or barium. (But remember, the caulks are *not* to solve gait problems!)

THE RACKING/ WALKING/FOX TROTTING HORSE

The Racking Horse, who is often too square or trotty, may be shod as described above to break him out of trot into a rack. While more animation and higher action is sought in the Racking Horse, it is better to go with regular weight shoes and normal angles and have a lower-action, natural rack than it is to use exaggerated weights and angles and risk injury or unsoundness.

A pacey Tennessee Walking Horse who is going to be shown is a somewhat different matter from trying to change a regular pace into a single-foot gait, because you're trying to obtain a good head-nodding run-walk, with speed. To facilitate a good show ring gait, the angle of both the front and back feet is kept high, while the toe is kept short. Heavy shoes—perhaps even "plantation" shoes—may be used in front. Lighter shoes, even training weight plates, are placed on the hind feet. Once shod this way, the horse must be trained and brought up to speed gradually, or there is a good chance he will take up a very hard pace.

The same type of shoeing as above, using regular-weight shoes, is often useful for ambling horses.

A fox trotter who tends to pace, or who does a running walk, can be shod using the 52/front and 55-60/hind degree formula, adjusting this until the horse does a good head-shaking flat walk and a properly timed fox.

LONG-TERM SOLUTIONS

Regardless of the desired gait, farriers should never neglect good fundamental shoeing principles. The shoe must be an appropriate size for the foot, and support it all the way around to the quarters and the heels. The hoof angle should never vary more than 3 degrees from the natural angle of the foot. Even then, when angles are changed, the horse should be allowed a few days to adjust to it (unridden) until his tendons become accustomed. Shoe calks, toe weights, special shoes and training devices are, at best, short-term answers to gait problems. The best long-term solutions to such problems is to breed horses with naturally good intermediate gaits and bring them along as slowly—and naturally—as possible.

—Appendix III—

Below are the names, addresses and phone numbers of associations that represent various breeds and types of gaited saddle horses. Also listed are the titles of their official publications, if any. For up-to-date information regarding gaited horses, or to learn how to register a horse, contact the appropriate association.

American Association of Owners and Breeders of Peruvian Paso Horses
P.O. Box 30723
Oakland, CA 94604
Ph. 415/636-1049
AAOBPPH NEWSLETTER

American Saddlebred Horse Association
4093 Iron Works Pike
Lexington, KY 40511
Ph. 606/259-2742
THE AMERICAN SADDLEBRED

Florida Cracker Horse Assoc.
P.O. Box 186
Newberry, FL 32669
Ph. 904/472-2228

Golden American Saddlebred Horse Association, Inc.
Rt. 1, Box 67
Oxford Junction, IA 52323
Ph. 319/486-2072
GASHA NEWSLETTER

Half Saddlebred Registry
319 S. 6th St.
Coshocton, OH 43812-2119
Ph. 614/622-1012

International Racking Horse Breeders' & Exhibitors' Assoc.
P.O. Box 2434
Chattanooga, TN 37409
Ph. 615/756-9632

Kentucky Mountain Saddle Horse Association
P.O. Box 505
Irvine, KY 40336
Ph. 606/723-6551

McCurdy Plantation Horse Association
1020 Houston Rd.
Selma, AL 36701
Ph. 334/872-5412

Missouri Fox Trotting Horse Breed Association, Inc.
P.O. Box 1027
Ava, MO 65608-1027
Ph. 417/683-2468
MISSOURI FOX TROTTING JOURNAL

Mountain Pleasure Horse Association
P.O. Box 670
Paris, KY 40362-0670
MPHA NEWS

National Spotted Saddle Horse Association
P.O. Box 898
108 N. Spring St.
Murfreesboro, TN 37133-0898
Ph. 615/890-2864
NATIONAL SPOTTED SADDLE HORSE JOURNAL

North American Single-footing Horse Association
Box 1079
Three Forks, MT 59752
406/285-6826
4-BEAT

Paso Fino Horse Association, Inc.
100 W. Main; P.O. Box 600
Bowling Green, FL 33834-0600
Ph. 813/375-4331
PASO FINO HORSE WORLD

Peruvian Part-Blood Registry
2027 Cribbens St.
Boise, ID 83704
PPBR NEWSLETTER

Peruvian Paso Horse Registry of North America
1038 4th St., #4
Santa Rosa, CA 95404-4319
Ph. 707/579-4394
NUESTRO CABALLO

Peruvian Paso Part-Blood Registry
1038 4th St., #4
Santa Rosa, CA 95404-4319
Ph. 707/579-4394

Racking Horse Breeders Association of America
Rt. 2, Box 72-A
Decatur, AL 35603
Ph. 205/353-7225
THE RACKING HORSE REVIEW

Rocky Mountain Horse Association
1140 McCalls Mill Rd.
Lexington, KY 40515
Ph. 606/263-4374
ROCKY MOUNTAIN NEWSLETTER

Spotted Saddle Horse Breeder's & Exhibitors Association
P.O. Box 1046
Shelbyville, TN 37160
615/684-7496
SPOTTED SADDLE HORSE NEWS

Tennessee Walking Horse Breeders' and Exhibitors' Association
P.O. Box 286
Lewisburg, TN 37091-0286
Ph. 615/359-1574
VOICE OF THE TENNESSEE WALKING HORSE

Tiger Horse Association
404 Polk 47
Mena, AR 71953
Ph. 501/394-3746

United States Icelandic Horse Federation
38 Park St.
Montclair, NJ 07042
Ph. 201/783-3429
USIHF NEWSLETTER

Walkaloosa Horse Association
3815 N. Campbell Rd.
Otis Orchards, WA 99027
Ph. 509/926-7011
WALKALOOSA NEWS

Walking Horse Owners' Assn. of America
1535 W. Northfield Blvd. #3A
Murfreesboro, TN 37129
Ph. 615/890-9120
WHOA NEWS

—BIBLIOGRAPHY—

BOOKS:

Albright, Verne R.; *Horseback Across the Americas*; Forge Valley Books, Pasadena, CA

Albright, Verne R.; *The Peruvian Paso and His Classical Equitation*; Forge Valley Books, 1995; Pasadena, CA

American Horse Council; 1991-92 & 1995 *Horse Industry Directory*

Bennet, Deborah, Ph.D; *Principles of Conformation* (Books 1-3); Equus Publications, 1992

Crabtree, Helen; *Saddleseat Equitation*; Doubleday NY, 1982

Childs, Marilyn Carlson; *Riding Show Horses*; Arco, 1972

Dent, Anthony; *The Horse Through Fifty Centuries of Civilization*; Phaidon Press, Ltd., 1974

Downey, Bill; *Tom Bass, Black Horseman*; Saddle and Bridle, 1975

Dossenbach, Monique and Hans; *The Noble Horse*; Translated from German by Margaret Whale Sutton; G.K. Hall & Co., 1983

Fianoli, Luigi; *Horses and Horsemanship Through the Ages*; Crown Publishers, Inc. NY, 1969

Geddes, Candida (Edited by); *The Complete Book of the Horse*; Octopus Books, Ltd., London, 1978

Goodall, Daphne Maichin; *Horses of the World*; Macmillan, 1973

Green, Ben A.; *Biography of the Tennessee Walking Horse*; The Parthenon Press, 1960

Hartley, E. Edwards and Macgregor-Morris, Pamela; THE HORSE; Longmeadow Press, 1987

Isenbugel, Dr. Ewald, and Jonsonn, Marit; *Icelandic Horses*; The International Federation of Icelandic Horse Associations (FEIF), 1986

Jonsson, Marit; *Judging Icelandic Breeding Horses*; The International Federation of Icelandic Horse Associations (FEIF); 1988

Kays, John M.; *The Horse*, 3rd Edition; Arco Publishing, 1982

LaHood, George J., and MacWilliam, Rosalie; *The American Paso Fino*, published by authors, 1976

Littauer, Vladimir S.; *The Development of Modern Riding*; Howell Book House, 1991

Magnusson, Sigurdur A; *Stallion of the North*; Longship Press, 1978

Oetinger, Judy Fisher; *The Saddlebred*; 1991 (published by author)

Roberts, David, and Krakaner, Jon; *Iceland, Land of the Sagas*; Harry N. Abrams, Inc., NY, 1990

Schwartz, Christine; *The Joy of Icelandics: A Training Guide*; Icelandic Horse Farm, Site 20, Comp 9 R.R. 1, Vernon, BC VIT 6L4, Canada (order info: 604/545-2336)

Warren, Evans James; *Horse*; W.H. Freeman & Co., 1977

Womack, Dr. Bob; *Echoes of Hoofbeats*; Middle Tennessee State University; Walking Horse Publications; Shelbyville TN, 1973

MAGAZINES:

The American Saddlebred
4093 Iron Works Pike
Lexington, KY 40511-8434
Ph. 606/259-2742

HEAVENLY GAITS

Blue Ribbon (no longer published)

Brio International
P.O. Box 102, North Rd.
Bridgton, ME 04009-0102
Ph. 207/647-2712

Caballo
P.O. Box 1049
Lake Elsinore, CA 92531
Ph. 714/272-3791

Conquistador
8729 Santa Rosa Rd.
Buellton, CA
805/686-4616

Equus
656 Quince Orchard Rd.
Gaithersburg, MD 20878-1472
Ph. 301-977-3900

4-Beat
P.O. Box 1079
Three Forks, MT 59752
Ph. 406/285-6826

Favorite Gait
P.O. Box 1472
Jackson, MS 39215-1472

Horse and Horseman
34249 Camino Capistrano
Capistrano Beach, CA 92624

Horse Illustrated
P.O. Box 6050
Mission Viejo, CA 92690-6050
Ph. 714/855-8822

The Journal
P.O. Box 1027
Ava, MO 65608-1027
Ph. 417/683-2468

National Spotted Saddle Horse Journal
P.O. Box 898
Murfreesboro, TN 37133-0898
Ph. 615/890-2864

North American Walker
60 Carranza Rd.
Tabernacle, NJ 08088
Ph. 609/268-2628

Nuestro Caballo
1038 4th St., #4
Santa Rosa, CA 95404-4319
Ph. 707/579-4394

Paso Fino Horse World
101 N. Collins St.
Plant City, FL 33566-3311
Ph. 813-719-7777

Racking Review
P.O. Box 777
104 Public Square
Waynesboro, TN 38485
Ph. 615/722-3688

HEAVENLY GAITS

The Review of the Spotted Saddle Horse
7297 Delina Rd.
Petersburg, TN 37144
Ph. 615/659-9602

Saddle & Bridle
375 N. Jackson
St. Louis, MO 63130-4243
Ph. 314/725-9115

Spotted Saddle Horse News
P.O. Box 909
Shelbyville, TN 37160
Ph. 615/389-9386

Voice of the Tennessee Walking Horse
P.O. Box 286
250 N. Ellington Parkway
Lewisburg, TN 37091-0286
Ph. 615/359-1567

Walking Horse Report
P.O. Box 1007
Shelbyville, TN 37160-1007
Ph. 615/684-8123

TAPES:

The Gaits of Horses; Ted Sare Productions; 1991

A Look into the Past, Early Great Horses of the Breed; Middle Tennessee
State University

Horses of Kirkjubar; 1979

INDEX

HEAVENLY GAITS

H

M

V

Valerie Emerald   48
Van Lennep, Frances Dodge   53
Van Meter's Waxy   33
Varnon's Roebuck   33
Vaszuez, Anibal   152
Volare   182, 185

W

walk   13
Walkaloosa   206
Walkaloosa Horse, photo   206
Walker, Fred   89
Walker, Jami/Brooke, photo   *119*
Walker, John   85
Walker, Rex, photo   *108*
Walker's Allen   85
Walking Horse Trainers' Association   105
Walton, Winona   192
Warden, Margaret Lindsley   89
Wartrace, Tennessee   77, 87
Washington Denmark   76
West Indies   30, 177
Western States Celebration, The   106
Whip   71
White Star   84
Wilson Allen   112
Wilson's Allen   80, 81, 110
Wilson, Frank   81
Wing Commander   47
Wing Commander, photo   48
Wiser, Winston   89
Wiser's Dimples   110
Womack, Dr. Bob   89

X

Xenophon   169

Y

Z